A GUIDE TO

OTHELLO

The Shakespeare Handbooks

Guides available now:

- Antony and Cleopatra
- As You Like It
- The Comedy of Errors
- Coriolanus
- Cymbeline
- Hamlet
- Henry IV, Part 1
- Henry IV, Part 2
- Julius Caesar
- King Lear
- Love's Labour's Lost
- Macbeth
- Measure for Measure
- The Merchant of Venice
- The Merry Wives of Windsor
- A Midsummer Night's Dream
- Much Ado About Nothing
- Othello
- Pericles
- Richard II
- Richard III
- Romeo and Juliet
- The Tempest
- Twelfth Night
- The Winter's Tale

Further titles in preparation.

The Shakespeare Handbooks

A Guide to
Othello

by Alistair McCallum

Upstart Crow Publications

First published in 2018 by
Upstart Crow Publications

A CIP catalogue record for this book
is available from the British Library

ISBN 978 1 899747 12 2

www.shakespeare-handbooks.com

Setting the scene

Othello was probably written in the period 1602-4, when Shakespeare was in his late thirties. He was a leading member of England's foremost acting company, based at the Globe Theatre in London. With the death of Queen Elizabeth in 1603, the company came under the patronage of her successor, King James I, a great theatre enthusiast, and became known as the King's Men.

The first recorded performance of *Othello* was at the new king's court in 1604. The play was an immediate and continuing success. Many of Shakespeare's plays were later adapted in various ways to suit current tastes – for example, songs might be added, or even endings changed – but *Othello* remained enduringly popular in its original form after the playwright's death in 1616.

In 1642, with civil war looming, Parliament ordered all London's theatres to be closed: it was not until 1660, with the restoration of King Charles II, that this ban was lifted. One of the first productions to celebrate the reopening of the theatres was a staging of *Othello* in December of that year. The part of Desdemona was played by Margaret Hughes, in what was almost certainly the first performance by a woman on an English stage; before this, women's parts had been played exclusively by boys.

Set against a background of feverish political and military activity, the tragedy of *Othello* is intimate and compelling. Overflowing with rich, musical, stately language, it is a drama that involves its audience intensely:

"Of all Shakespeare's tragedies, Othello *is the most painfully exciting and the most terrible ... the reader's heart and mind are held in a vice, experiencing the extremes of pity and fear, sympathy and repulsion, sickening hope and dreadful expectation ... Nowhere else in Shakespeare do we hold our breath in such anxiety and for so long a time as in the later acts of* Othello.*"*

A. C. Bradley, *Shakespearean Tragedy*, 1904

Runaway lovers

In the wealthy, opulent republic of Venice, a secret marriage has taken place.

The newlyweds are Desdemona, the young daughter of a Venetian senator, and Othello, a Moorish general who has long served the republic as a military commander. Having eloped in the dead of night, the couple are now at a nearby inn.

News of the marriage has just emerged. Roderigo, a rich, dissolute young Venetian, is dismayed; he had been hoping to marry the beautiful Desdemona himself, and he is appalled at her match with the ageing, dark-skinned foreign soldier.

Curtain up

Iago bears a grudge

Roderigo is angrily confronting Iago, Othello's aide and trusted adviser, believing that he knew in advance about the Moor's plan to elope with Desdemona. He is furious that Iago, who has often benefited from Roderigo's generosity, did not warn him about the marriage.

For his part, Iago vehemently denies any knowledge of Othello's decision:

Roderigo: Tush, never tell me, I take it much unkindly
That thou, Iago, who hast had my purse
As if the strings were thine, shouldst know of this.
Iago: 'Sblood,[1] but you'll not hear me. If ever I did dream
Of such a matter, abhor me.

[1] *God's blood*

Iago goes on to assure Roderigo that he hates the Moor, just as Roderigo himself does. His animosity, he explains, is due to Othello's recent failure to promote him to the post of lieutenant. Iago knew himself to be the best man for the job, and was supported by influential Venetians, but Othello refused his request for promotion with evasive answers:

Iago: Three great ones of the city,
In personal suit[1] to make me his lieutenant,
Off-capped to him, and by the faith of man
I know my price, I am worth no worse a place.
But he, as loving his own pride and purposes,
Evades them, with a bombast circumstance[2]
Horribly stuffed with epithets of war,[3]
And in conclusion
Nonsuits[4] my mediators.

[1] *appeal, petition*
[2] *in formal, convoluted language*
[3] *padded out with military jargon*
[4] *refuses, rejects*

It finally emerged that the general had already chosen another man as his lieutenant. To Iago's disgust, that man was Michael Cassio, a Florentine whose military experience is insignificant in comparison with Iago's:

Iago: Mere prattle without practice [1]
Is all his soldiership – but he, sir, had th'election
And I, of whom his [2] eyes had seen the proof
At Rhodes, at Cyprus and on other grounds,
Christian and heathen, must be be-leed [3] …

[1] *empty chatter without practical knowledge*
[2] *Othello's*
[3] *left high and dry*

Iago must resign himself to remaining in his current post, as the general's 'ancient' or standard-bearer. He has been a victim of favouritism, and has not received his rightful reward, he claims; it is not surprising that he hates Othello.

Roderigo asks Iago why he still follows the Moor. It is not out of a sense of duty, Iago answers; only a fool would spend his life obediently serving a master with nothing to show for it. Iago is happy to give the impression of devotion and loyalty, but it is purely his own profit that motivates him, and he intends to take advantage of the relationship. True feelings must be kept hidden, he insists. If they are revealed, the result can be dangerous:

Iago: In following him I follow but myself …
For when my outward action doth demonstrate
The native act and figure of my heart
In complement extern,[1] 'tis not long after
But I will wear my heart upon my sleeve [2]
For daws [3] to peck at: I am not what I am.[4]

[1] *if my appearance and behaviour reflected the secret activity of my heart*
[2] *my true feelings would soon be exposed*
[3] *jackdaws*
[4] *I am not what I seem to other people*

The alarm is raised

Iago urges Roderigo to wake Desdemona's father, the senator Brabantio, and warn him of his daughter's clandestine marriage.

The two men approach Brabantio's house. Roderigo's attempts to rouse the senator are drowned out by Iago's urgent, forceful cries:

Roderigo: What ho! Brabantio, Signior Brabantio, ho!
Iago: Awake, what ho, Brabantio! Thieves, thieves, thieves!
Look to your house, your daughter and your bags!
Thieves, thieves!

Brabantio appears at the balcony, ill-tempered at being summoned in the middle of the night. Again Iago takes the lead, brazenly hinting to the senator that his daughter is coupled with a dark, evil spirit:

Iago: … for shame put on your gown!
Your heart is burst, you have lost half your soul,
Even now, now, very now, an old black ram
Is tupping[1] your white ewe! Arise, arise,
Awake the snorting[2] citizens with the bell
Or else the devil will make a grandsire[3] of you …

[1] *copulating with*
[2] *snoring*
[3] *grandfather*

When Brabantio learns that one of the men outside his window is Roderigo, he is displeased; he disapproves of the young gentleman, and has previously ordered him to stay away from his daughter. Roderigo tries unsuccessfully to reassure Brabantio that he has the senator's interests at heart.

Iago then interrupts, and his crude warnings immediately attract Brabantio's attention:

Iago: Because we come to do you service, and you think we are ruffians, you'll have your daughter covered [1] with a Barbary [2] horse; you'll have your nephews [3] neigh to you …
Brabantio: What profane wretch art thou?
Iago: I am one, sir, that comes to tell you your daughter and the Moor are now making the beast with two backs.[4]

[1] *mated*
[2] *from north Africa*
[3] *grandchildren, descendants*
[4] *copulating*

Roderigo now spells out what has happened: under cover of darkness, Brabantio's daughter Desdemona has secretly fled the house to be with Othello. Brabantio is shocked, and calls for his servants to bring him light and to search the house immediately.

As Brabantio goes back indoors, Iago tells Roderigo that he cannot stay; if he were seen to be one of his master's accusers, his position would be at risk. War is imminent, and Othello's services will be essential to Venice regardless of his misdemeanour. Iago, in turn, will be required to serve the general, and he cannot afford to lose his livelihood.

A search party will inevitably be raised when it is discovered that Desdemona is missing. Iago tells Roderigo the name of the inn where Othello will be found, then sets off to join his master.

At this point Brabantio comes out to join Roderigo. The house has been searched, and Desdemona is nowhere to be found. The senator is beside himself with anxiety and grief:

Brabantio: … gone she is,
And what's to come of my despised time
Is nought but bitterness. Now Roderigo,
Where didst thou see her? – O unhappy girl! –
With the Moor, say'st thou? – Who would be a father? –
How didst thou know 'twas she? – O, she deceives me
Past thought! – What said she to you?

Brabantio suspects that magical powers of some sort have been used on his daughter, and he now wishes that he had looked more favourably on Roderigo's attempts to court Desdemona. When Roderigo reveals that he can help to find the fugitive couple, Brabantio promises that he will be rewarded generously.

In all their heated arguments, Iago, Roderigo and Brabantio do not once mention Othello by name during the opening scenes:

"The term 'Moor' was an elastic one in the early modern period, used variously as a marker of race, geography, nationality, religion, or some combination of these. The term is associated in texts of the period with light-skinned Arabs from north-Africa; with dark-skinned sub-Saharan Africans; with Muslims from the Iberian Peninsula; and with the smaller number of men and women of color who lived in England, some as slaves and others as paid workers … By replacing Othello's name with the indeterminate sobriquet 'Moor', the general's opponents deny his individuality and insist instead on his role as a potentially threatening outsider."

Jessica Slights, Introduction to *Othello,* Internet Shakespeare Editions, 2018

Othello is summoned

Iago has joined Othello outside the inn where he has taken up residence with his new wife. He explains to his master that he has just spoken with Brabantio. In Iago's version of events, he was so shocked at the old senator's attitude that he found it difficult to refrain from violently assaulting him:

Iago: Nine or ten times
I had thought t'have yerked him[1] here, under the ribs.
Othello: 'Tis better as it is.
Iago: Nay, but he prated[2]
And spoke such scurvy and provoking terms
Against your honour,
That with the little godliness I have
I did full hard forbear him.[3]

1 *I was tempted to stab him*
2 *chattered foolishly*
3 *I spared him, with great difficulty*

Iago then turns to another subject. Brabantio is a very influential man in Venetian society, he points out, and he may be able to annul Othello's marriage, particularly if it has not yet been consummated.

Othello is unmoved. He knows that his usefulness to Venice as a military leader will far outweigh any qualms people may have over his marriage to the senator's daughter. Besides, he points out, he is of royal descent himself, even though this is not widely known in Venice, and is worthy of a bride such as Desdemona.

A group of men approaches through the darkness. Iago, believing this to be Brabantio and his search party, warns Othello to go inside. The general refuses, determined to stand his ground.

As the group comes closer, however, it becomes clear that this is not Brabantio and his followers; it is Othello's new lieutenant Cassio, accompanied by servants of the Duke of Venice himself. Their message is urgent: Othello's presence is required immediately at a council of war. The island of Cyprus, a Venetian possession, is under threat:

Othello: The goodness of the night upon you, friends.
What is the news?
Cassio: The Duke does greet you, general,
And he requires your haste-post-haste[1] appearance,
Even on the instant.
Othello: What's the matter, think you?
Cassio: Something from Cyprus, as I may divine;
It is a business of some heat. The galleys
Have sent a dozen sequent[2] messengers
This very night, at one another's heels,
And many of the consuls,[3] raised and met,
Are at the Duke's already. You have been hotly
called for …

[1] *urgent (an instruction often written on letters)*
[2] *successive, following one another*
[3] *councillors, advisers*

Othello agrees to come at once, pausing only to hurry into the inn to take his leave of Desdemona. While he is gone, Cassio asks what Othello is doing at an inn rather than at home. Iago's reply is crude but enigmatic:

Cassio: Ancient, what makes he here?
Iago: Faith, he tonight hath boarded[1] a land carrack:[2]
If it prove lawful prize,[3] he's made for ever.
Cassio: I do not understand.
Iago: He's married.

[1] *gone on board, entered*
[2] *ship carrying treasure*
[3] *if he is legally entitled to his plunder*

Before Iago has time to give any more details, Othello returns.

Brabantio accuses Othello

Just as Othello is about to set off to join the Duke and his council of war, Brabantio arrives, still furious at the disappearance of his daughter. A gang of armed men, including Roderigo, is with him, and he immediately orders them to seize the Moor.

Weapons are drawn on both sides, but Othello remains calm. He respects the senator's age and wisdom, he says, and is ready to listen:

Othello: Keep up[1] your bright swords, for the dew will rust them.
Good signior, you shall more command with years
Than with your weapons.

[1] *put away*

> *Keep up your bright swords ...*
>
> *"Brabantio's party arrive, but the threatened brawl is at once averted ... Othello's slight contempt for these excited Venetians, who flash their nice new swords like toys, gives extra weight to his unforced authority."*
>
> John Wain, *The Living World of Shakespeare*, 1964

Brabantio launches into an angry denunciation of Othello. He accuses him of casting a spell on Desdemona, who has never shown any interest in marriage, and who would never otherwise have allowed herself to be abducted in this way:

Brabantio: Damned as thou art, thou hast enchanted her,
For I'll refer me to all things of sense,[1]
If she in chains of magic were not bound,
Whether a maid so tender, fair and happy,
So opposite to marriage that she shunned
The wealthy, curled[2] darlings of our nation,
Would ever have, t'incur a general mock,
Run from her guardage[3] to the sooty bosom
Of such a thing as thou?

[1] *I would present my case to anyone with any degree of perception*
[2] *elegant, stylish*
[3] *would ever have abandoned her protectors, making herself an object of ridicule*

The senator orders his men to arrest Othello on suspicion of sorcery, and to keep him in prison until a trial can be arranged. Othello, still calm, points out that the Duke, who has summoned him urgently, might be displeased.

Brabantio is shocked to hear that a council of war has been called in the middle of the night. He will need to join the Duke himself, but he insists that his case against Othello must still be considered:

Brabantio: How? The Duke in council?
In this time of the night? Bring him away:[1]
Mine's not an idle cause, the Duke himself,
Or any of my brothers of the state,[2]
Cannot but feel this wrong as 'twere their own.
For if such actions may have passage free[3]
Bond-slaves and pagans shall our statesmen be.

[1] *bring Othello with us*
[2] *fellow-senators*
[3] *are allowed to go unchallenged*

Although *Othello* is a fictional story, it is set against the background of the struggle between Venice and the Ottoman Empire (which included modern-day Turkey and Greece, as well as vast stretches of territory in the Middle East and Africa) for control of the Mediterranean Sea. This conflict culminated in the major sea-battle of Lepanto in 1571.

In Shakespeare's day, this battle, won decisively by the Venetians and their allies, was well within living memory. It was known to be a subject that interested the new patron of Shakespeare's acting company, King James I:

"Othello *probably owes something to the king's known interest in the Christian struggle against the Muslim Turks; in his youth, James had written a 'celestial poem',* Lepanto, *to celebrate the great sea-battle of 1571 in which a Christian fleet organised by the Venetian republic and captained by Don John of Austria virtually destroyed Muslim sea-power. Clearly the play evokes that period and the tensions that led up to the battle; the Mediterranean is where conflicting religions meet, a cosmopolitan mixing-pot where an alien like the Moor might plausibly make his mark."*

Richard Dutton, *William Shakespeare: A Literary Life*, 1989

A threat to Venice

I, iii

In a chamber in the Duke's palace, the council of war is under way. Although reports are inconsistent, there seems to be little doubt that a large Turkish fleet is heading for the Venetian island of Cyprus.

A sailor rushes in with more news: the fleet has been seen sailing towards the island of Rhodes. The Duke and his councillors are not convinced: Rhodes is better defended than Cyprus, and is of less importance to the Turks.

It soon becomes clear that the fleet has indeed been to Rhodes, but only to join up with reinforcements. A Turkish armada is now heading directly for Cyprus, and Montano, the Venetian governor of the island, has asked for urgent assistance.

Othello, Brabantio and their followers now arrive. The Duke immediately informs Othello that he will be needed in the imminent battle with the Turks.

Brabantio, on the other hand, is interested only in the ill-treatment of his daughter. Despite the urgency of the situation, the Duke and his councillors listen sympathetically:

Brabantio: … my particular grief
Is of so flood-gate [1] and o'erbearing nature
That it engluts [2] and swallows other sorrows
And it is still itself.
Duke: Why? What's the matter?
Brabantio: My daughter, O my daughter!
Senator: Dead?
Brabantio: Ay, to me:
She is abused, stolen from me and corrupted
By spells and medicines bought of mountebanks [3] …

[1] *torrential, overwhelming*
[2] *consumes, devours*
[3] *quack doctors, fraudsters*

Brabantio insists that witchcraft must have been used to seduce Desdemona. This is an extremely serious charge, says the Duke: even if the culprit were his own son, the appropriate punishment would be death. The council is shocked when Brabantio reveals that the man in question is Othello, their trusted general.

A love story

Othello respectfully addresses the Duke and the assembled council. It is true that he has married Desdemona, he announces. He then reminds his listeners that he has been a soldier since he was virtually a child, and apologises for his lack of eloquence:

Othello: … little of this great world can I speak
More than pertains to feats of broil [1] and battle,
And therefore little shall I grace my cause
In speaking for myself. Yet, by your gracious patience,
I will a round unvarnished tale deliver
Of my whole course of love …

[1] *turmoil, upheaval*

Brabantio, unable to contain his anger and disbelief, interrupts impatiently. It is inconceivable that his daughter has married the Moor of her own free will:

Brabantio: A maiden never bold,
Of spirit so still and quiet that her motion
Blushed at herself; [1] and she, in spite of nature,
Of years, of country, credit, [2] everything,
To fall in love with what she feared to look on?

[1] *any stirring of her feelings made her blush*
[2] *in spite of differences of character, age, nationality and reputation*

He repeats his accusation that Othello has used witchcraft – probably in the form of magical potions – to influence his daughter. The Duke points out that Brabantio's suspicions do not amount to genuine evidence. One of the senators turns to Othello and asks him directly whether he has used any kind of deception to win Desdemona's affections.

Othello proposes that they ask Desdemona herself, and the Duke sends for her. In the meantime, Othello volunteers to describe how the two of them fell in love. He recounts how he had often visited Desdemona's father Brabantio, who admired Othello and loved to hear of his exploits and his travels:

Othello: … I spake of most disastrous chances,[1]
Of moving accidents by flood and field,[2]
Of hair-breadth scapes i' th' imminent deadly
breach,[3]
Of being taken by the insolent foe
And sold to slavery …
… of the cannibals that each other eat,
The Anthropophagi,[4] and men whose heads
Do grow beneath their shoulders.

[1] *unlucky, ill-starred events*
[2] *stirring incidents at sea and on the battlefield*
[3] *narrow escapes from death under a break in the overhanging battlements*
[4] *man-eaters*

Desdemona would take every opportunity that she could to listen as Othello and her father talked. Eventually, with Othello's encouragement, she asked to spend some time alone with him. She was deeply touched by his stories of the hardships he had endured, and Othello in turn was moved by her concern:

Othello: My story being done
She gave me for my pains a world of sighs,
She swore in faith 'twas strange, 'twas passing[1]
strange,
'Twas pitiful, 'twas wondrous pitiful …
… She loved me for the dangers I had passed
And I loved her that[2] she did pity them.
This only is the witchcraft I have used.

[1] *exceptionally*
[2] *for the fact that, because*

Brabantio accepts defeat

The Duke, affected by Othello's account, remarks that it is not surprising that Desdemona has fallen in love. He advises Brabantio to accept the situation rather than fight hopelessly against it.

Desdemona herself now arrives at the council. Brabantio, confident that he will be proved correct, asks her to say publicly where her loyalties lie. He does not receive the answer he had anticipated:

Brabantio: Do you perceive, in all this noble company,
Where most you owe obedience?
Desdemona: My noble father,
I do perceive here a divided duty.
To you I am bound for life and education:[1]
My life and education both do learn[2] me
How to respect you; you are the lord of duty,
I am hitherto your daughter.[3] But here's my husband:
And so much duty as my mother showed
To you, preferring you before her father,
So much I challenge that I may profess
Due to the Moor my lord.[4]

1 *I am indebted to you for my life and upbringing*
2 *teach*
3 *until now, my identity has been as your daughter*
4 *I claim the same right to place my husband above my father*

Brabantio accepts his daughter's declaration, but he remains resentful. He wishes he had never fathered a child, he claims; and although he gives his blessing to the marriage, he makes no secret of the fact that he wishes it had never happened.

> *"Before Desdemona's first appearance in the play we hear several conflicting accounts of her ... Her measured sentences immediately modify previous impressions; she is neither headstrong nor bewitched, nor merely the impulsive, romantic and apparently motherless girl described by Othello. On the contrary, she confronts her angry father and later the Duke with complete presence of mind ..."*
>
> E. A. J. Honigmann, Introduction to the Arden edition of *Othello*, 1999

The Duke advises his senator to take a more philosophical attitude. Now that Brabantio's worst fears have been confirmed, there is nothing to be gained from brooding over the past:

Duke: When remedies are past,[1] the griefs are ended
By seeing the worst which late on hopes depended.[2]
To mourn a mischief that is past and gone
Is the next[3] way to draw new mischief on.

[1] *when there is no further hope of a remedy*
[2] *by the fact that we have seen the worst happen, bringing our previous hopes to an end*
[3] *nearest, quickest*

Brabantio is not consoled by the Duke's advice. He remarks cynically that the Venetians would surely not take the same stoical view if Cyprus were lost to the Turks. However, he is now resigned to his daughter's marriage, and he asks the Duke and his council to continue with their discussions.

The Duke now turns to Othello. Although the current governor of Cyprus is undoubtedly competent, he says, the consensus throughout Venice is that Othello is the best man for the job in these dangerous times. It has been decided that he should take charge of the island and deal with the threatened Turkish invasion.

The Duke regrets that the general's new appointment should be made so soon after the wedding, but Othello is untroubled. War has become his natural environment, and he relishes the prospect of being in the thick of battle once more:

Othello: The tyrant custom,[1] most grave senators,
Hath made the flinty and steel couch of war
My thrice-driven[2] bed of down.

[1] *habit, which rules resolutely over our lives*
[2] *extremely soft, luxurious*

Othello has only one request to make: he wants suitable accommodation to be provided for Desdemona. The Duke misunderstands, assuming that she is to stay behind with her father. Othello corrects him; he wishes his wife to accompany him on his expedition.

For his part, Brabantio, still upset, does not want his daughter to remain in his house. Desdemona now speaks up for herself:

Desdemona: … if I be left behind,
A moth[1] of peace, and he go to the war,
The rites for which I love him are bereft me,[2]
And I a heavy interim shall support[3]
By his dear absence. Let me go with him.

[1] *an idle, worthless creature*
[2] *the rights and honours of marriage will be denied me*
[3] *I will endure a long and difficult wait*

Othello asks the Duke to grant Desdemona her wish. He is no longer young, he points out, and it is not merely out of sexual desire that he wants his wife to be with him. Besides, he assures the Duke, he would never allow his personal pleasures to interfere with the serious business of war.

Becoming impatient, the Duke says that Othello and Desdemona must do as they please. The expedition to Cyprus is urgent, and Othello must set off this very night. Othello asks his trusted aide Iago to remain behind and accompany Desdemona when she is ready to join him on the island.

The meeting now breaks up. The Duke tries to reassure Brabantio that Othello will make a worthy husband for his daughter, but the old senator remains gloomy about their prospects:

Duke: … noble signior,
If virtue no delighted beauty lack [1]
Your son-in-law is far more fair than black.[2]
Brabantio: … Look to [3] her, Moor, if thou hast eyes to see:
She has deceived her father, and may thee.

[1] *if good qualities signify delightful beauty*
[2] *good-natured rather than evil*
[3] *watch, keep an eye on*

Evil intentions

Eventually, only Roderigo and Iago remain in the council chamber. Roderigo is dismayed that the beautiful Desdemona, whom he had admired and pursued so zealously, has clearly fallen in love with the Moor, and their marriage is a reality. He confides in Iago that he is tempted to drown himself.

Iago pours scorn on his companion's self-pity. Roderigo argues that his feelings are so strong that he cannot control them, but Iago dismisses his claim impatiently.

People are responsible for their own emotions, insists Iago, and should use reason and willpower to curb their baser instincts, including love:

Iago: … 'tis in ourselves[1] that we are thus, or thus. Our bodies are gardens, to the which our wills are gardeners … we have reason to cool our raging motions,[2] our carnal stings, our unbitted[3] lusts; whereof I take this, that you call love, to be a sect or scion.[4]

[1] *within our own power*
[2] *our reason enables us to control our violent impulses*
[3] *unbridled*
[4] *cutting or offshoot*

To escape from his state of misery, says Iago, Roderigo must pull himself together and make up his mind to seduce Desdemona. To do this, he will need to amass as much money as he can and travel to Cyprus, in disguise, with the Venetian fleet.

Othello and Desdemona will soon tire of one another, and Roderigo must be prepared to take advantage of the situation. Above all, he needs to sell off all his assets for ready money:

Iago: Put money in thy purse, follow thou the wars, defeat thy favour with an usurped beard[1] … It cannot be that Desdemona should long continue her love to the Moor – put money in thy purse – nor he his to her. It was a violent commencement in her, and thou shalt see an answerable sequestration[2] – put but money in thy purse. These Moors are changeable in their wills …

[1] *disfigure your appearance with a false beard*
[2] *her love started suddenly and impetuously, and will have a similarly abrupt conclusion*

There is to be no more talk of drowning. If Roderigo is to die young, it should only be as punishment for achieving his aim:

Iago: A pox of drowning thyself … seek thou rather to be hanged in compassing thy joy [1] than to be drowned and go without her.

[1] *satisfying your desire for Desdemona*

Iago promises to support Roderigo in his quest; after all, he hates the Moor, as he has already told Roderigo, and would be glad to see him betrayed. Roderigo leaves, vowing to sell all his property, and the two men agree to meet again in the morning.

Now that Iago is alone, his contempt for Roderigo becomes clear; he maintains a pretence of friendship solely in order to dupe the young gentleman out of his money. Iago's thoughts quickly move to his chief preoccupation, his hatred of Othello. He suspects that the general has had an affair with his wife Emilia:

Iago: I hate the Moor
And it is thought abroad [1] that 'twixt my sheets
He's done my office.[2] I know not if't be true,
But I for mere suspicion in that kind
Will do as if for surety.[3]

[1] *widely, generally*
[2] *taken my place; slept with my wife*
[3] *will act as if I knew it to be true*

> *"Iago believes in will-power. One can make everything of oneself, and of other people. Others, too, are only an instrument. They can be moulded like clay. Iago despises people even more than he hates them."*
>
> Jan Kott, *Shakespeare Our Contemporary*, 1964

Another source of resentment, Othello's choice of Cassio as his lieutenant, now comes into Iago's mind. Thinking quickly, he comes up with a plan to wound both men. Cassio is a handsome man, and attractive to women; it would not be difficult to convince Othello that an illicit relationship had developed between his lieutenant and Desdemona. The result is likely to be devastating:

Iago: The Moor is of a free and open nature
That thinks men honest that but[1] seem to be so,
And will as tenderly[2] be led by th' nose
As asses are.
I have't, it is engendered![3] Hell and night
Must bring this monstrous birth to the world's light.

[1] *only, merely*
[2] *gently, tamely*
[3] *conceived, created*

Cyprus is saved II, i

A storm is raging in the seas around Cyprus. The island's governor, Montano, and two of his attendants are looking out intently from a headland, trying to see signs of the Turkish fleet.

They are hopeful that the violent storm has put an end to the Turkish invasion, and their hopes are confirmed when news arrives that the enemy's fleet has been severely damaged. The message has come from Othello's lieutenant Cassio, who has just arrived on the island.

Cassio himself now approaches. Although he is thankful that the Turkish fleet has been scattered, he is concerned for the safety of his general, having lost sight of Othello's ship in the storm. Montano and the others decide to go down to the harbour to keep a lookout, but at the same moment shouting and cheering suddenly erupt in the distance: another ship has just arrived.

It is not Othello's ship, however, but that of Iago, who is accompanying Desdemona. Cassio is joyful at the ship's safe arrival, and marvels at the speed with which they have travelled, overtaking the general himself. He is effusive in his admiration for Othello's young wife:

Cassio: Tempests themselves, high seas, and howling winds,
The guttered rocks and congregated sands,[1]
Traitors ensteeped to clog the guiltless keel,[2]
As having sense of beauty, do omit
Their mortal natures,[3] letting go safely by
The divine Desdemona.

[1] *jagged rocks and sandbanks*
[2] *treacherous underwater traps for unsuspecting ships*
[3] *renounce their deadly activities, as if they had an appreciation of beauty*

Desdemona now arrives, escorted by Iago and his wife Emilia. Roderigo, who has come to Cyprus with the aim of seducing Desdemona, is also with them. Cassio greets Desdemona warmly and extravagantly:

Cassio: O, behold,
The riches of the ship is come on shore:
You men of Cyprus, let her have your knees! [1]
Hail to thee, lady, and the grace of heaven,
Before, behind thee, and on every hand
Enwheel[2] thee round!

[1] *kneel before her*
[2] *encircle*

> *"Desdemona enters ... for a thrilling instant, her radiance transforms all that lies about her. Then she descends, Cassio painting her once again in great brush strokes of legend, as if it were the homecoming of some divinity. Should we perhaps remember here that Cyprus is the ancient home of Aphrodite?"*
>
> Maynard Mack, *Everybody's Shakespeare*, 1993

Iago takes liberties

Desdemona asks anxiously for news of her husband. Cassio tries to reassure her that he is expected to arrive soon, and as they talk shouting is again heard from the harbour; another Venetian ship has arrived. Cassio sends an attendant to investigate. He then greets Iago and, with self-conscious gallantry, kisses his wife Emilia. Iago responds mockingly:

Cassio: Welcome, mistress.
Let it not gall your patience,[1] good Iago,
That I extend my manners;[2] 'tis my breeding
That gives me this bold show of courtesy.
[*kisses Emilia*]
Iago: Sir, would she give you so much of her lips
As of her tongue she oft bestows on me[3]
You'd have enough.

1 *irritate you*
2 *that I greet your wife in this chivalrous way*
3 *if she kissed you as enthusiastically as she scolds me*

Iago continues to tease his wife. She manages to criticise him even when she is not speaking, he claims. Undeterred by his present company, he soon becomes blatantly crude about women in general:

Iago: … you are pictures[1] out of
doors, bells[2] in your parlours, wild-cats in your
kitchens, saints in your injuries, devils being
offended, players in your housewifery,[3] and
housewives[4] in your beds.
Desdemona: O, fie upon thee, slanderer!
Iago: Nay, it is true, or else I am a Turk:
You rise to play, and go to bed to work.

1 *models of virtue and beauty*
2 *noisy, jangling*
3 *careless when it comes to housekeeping*
4 *serious, hard-working*

Desdemona, doing her best to hide her anxiety about Othello, encourages Iago to come up with more of his sayings. He produces a series of couplets about various types of women and their determination to find a mate:

Iago: … If she be fair and wise, fairness and wit,[1]
The one's for use, the other useth it.[2]
Desdemona: Well praised. How if she be black[3] and witty?
Iago: If she be black, and thereto have a wit,
She'll find a white that shall her blackness fit.[4]
Desdemona: Worse and worse.
Emilia: How if fair and foolish?
Iago: She never yet was foolish that was fair,
For even her folly helped her to an heir.

[1] *good sense, astuteness*
[2] *her intelligence enables her to make use of her good looks*
[3] *dark-haired*
[4] *she'll find a man (a 'wight') to suit her*

Eventually Desdemona turns to Cassio. From a distance, Iago carefully notes their relaxed, friendly relationship:

Desdemona: Do not learn of him, Emilia, though he be thy husband. How say you, Cassio, is he not a most profane and liberal[1] counsellor?
Cassio: He speaks home,[2] madam, you may relish him more in[3] the soldier than in the scholar.
Iago: [*aside*] He takes her by the palm; ay, well said, whisper. With as little a web as this will I ensnare as great a fly as Cassio. Ay, smile upon her, do: I will gyve[4] thee in thine own courtesies.

[1] *irreverent and shameless*
[2] *he goes straight to the point*
[3] *in the role of*
[4] *shackle, trap*

The lovers are reunited

Othello himself finally arrives, and he and Desdemona greet one another devotedly:

Othello: If it were now to die[1]
'Twere now to be most happy, for I fear
My soul hath her content so absolute
That not another comfort like to this
Succeeds in unknown fate.[2]
Desdemona: The heavens forbid
But that our loves and comforts should increase
Even as our days do grow.
Othello: Amen to that, sweet powers!
I cannot speak enough of this content,
It stops me here,[3] it is too much of joy.

1 *if this were my time to die*
2 *no other happiness like this can follow in the unknown future that fate has in store for me*
3 *chokes me, makes me unable to speak*

As Othello and Desdemona embrace tenderly, Iago looks on malevolently; he will make sure that their happiness does not last.

If it were now to die ...

"Othello's reunion speech to Desdemona in Cyprus underlines this sense of a movement accomplished, a still point of happiness like the final scene of a comedy ... But at the same time that Othello celebrates his peak of joy so markedly, his invocations of death, fear, and unknown fate make us apprehensive about the post-comic future ... The happy ending is completed, but Othello and Desdemona are left to go on from there."

Susan Snyder, Othello *and the Conventions of Romantic Comedy*, 1972

Othello eventually turns to greet the others around him and confirms that, thanks to the storm, the Turkish threat is over. He is in good spirits, knowing that he is loved by the people of Cyprus and confident that Desdemona will be equally popular.

A setback for Roderigo

Othello and his wife depart for their new residence, and eventually only Iago and Roderigo are left. Iago wastes no time in informing Roderigo of the latest development: Desdemona has fallen passionately in love with Cassio, Othello's lieutenant.

Roderigo is shocked, and at first refuses to believe his companion. Iago insists that it is true: after all, he reminds him, Desdemona's love for the Moor arose suddenly, and it was only to be expected that she would quickly tire of him. The stories that first enchanted her have no doubt become dreary, and the Moor, ageing and unattractive as he is, cannot hold her interest for long.

It is not surprising that Desdemona, who is clearly a refined and sophisticated woman, should turn instead to the young, chivalrous Michael Cassio. He is cunning, claims Iago, and knows how to use his superficial charm to seduce women. Roderigo protests that Desdemona is too virtuous to be misled in this way, but Iago urges him not to be so innocent:

Iago: Didst thou not see her paddle with[1] the palm of his hand? Didst not mark that?
Roderigo: Yes, that I did, but that was but[2] courtesy.
Iago: Lechery, by this hand: an index and obscure prologue[3] to the history[4] of lust and foul thoughts. They met so near with their lips that their breaths embraced together.

[1] *fondle, play with*
[2] *only*
[3] *a secretive prelude*
[4] *the full story*

If Roderigo is to succeed in seducing Desdemona, Cassio must be removed. Iago explains that the young lieutenant is easily offended, and has a violent temper. If Roderigo manages to provoke him, there is every chance that Cassio will respond in an aggressive, ill-disciplined manner. Iago will then be able to stir up popular sentiment against him, and ensure that he is dismissed from his position.

Roderigo agrees to go along with the plan, and Iago promises to bring about suitable circumstances for inciting a quarrel with Cassio.

When Roderigo has left, Iago mulls over the situation. He is tormented by the suspicion that Othello has had an affair with his wife, and is determined to take his revenge:

Iago: … I do suspect the lusty Moor
Hath leaped into my seat,[1] the thought whereof
Doth like a poisonous mineral gnaw my inwards,[2]
And nothing can or shall content my soul
Till I am evened with him, wife for wife;
Or, failing so, yet that I put the Moor
At least into a jealousy so strong
That judgement[3] cannot cure …

1 *taken my place*
2 *innards, guts*
3 *rational thought*

Part of Iago's plan will involve the disgrace of Othello's lieutenant Cassio, in which the otherwise worthless Roderigo should prove useful. As yet, however, Iago's scheme is only half-formed:

Iago: 'Tis here, but yet confused:[1]
Knavery's plain face is never seen, till used.[2]

1 *the plan is in my head, but is still indistinct*
2 *wickedness does not become completely apparent until it is put into action*

Celebrations

Othello's herald reads a proclamation to the people of Cyprus, announcing a public holiday. There is to be unrestrained feasting and revelry, to celebrate the destruction of the Turkish fleet as well as Othello's marriage:

Herald: It is Othello's pleasure, our noble and valiant general, that, upon certain tidings now arrived, importing the mere perdition[1] of the Turkish fleet, every man put himself into triumph: some to dance, some to make bonfires, each man to what sport and revels his addiction leads him. For besides these beneficial news, it is the celebration of his nuptial …

[1] *total loss*

The festivities are to continue late into the night.

Both *Othello* (subtitled *The Moor of Venice*) and *The Merchant of Venice*, written a few years earlier, demonstrate Shakespeare's interest in the nature and experience of the stranger, the 'other'. This was a challenging theme at a time of great social division, when the state was still struggling to unite the nation under the relatively new Church of England:

"Like Shakespeare's other play with Venice in its title, Othello *is the story of an outsider. This would have had a profound impact on a contemporary audience. The whole machinery of church and state was geared to achieving uniformity of belief and action ... The only hope for an outsider is to make himself so useful that his services become indispensable – and this is what Othello has done."*

Nicholas Fogg, *Hidden Shakespeare*, 2013

An unwelcome invitation

Othello's lieutenant Cassio is to be in charge of security for the night. Othello tells him that, despite the boisterous atmosphere, it is important that those in positions of responsibility do not get too caught up in the celebrations:

Othello: Let's teach ourselves that honourable stop [1]
Not to outsport discretion.[2]

[1] *restraint, self-control*
[2] *not to go beyond the bounds dictated by our judgement*

He then retires for the night with Desdemona. Since their recent hasty elopement, their marriage has not yet been consummated:

Othello: Come, my dear love,
The purchase made, the fruits are to ensue:
That profit's yet to come 'tween me and you.

Iago now joins the lieutenant. Cassio remarks that it is time for them to take up their guard duties, but Iago assures him that there is no hurry. Othello has gone to bed earlier than usual, and for obvious reasons, he points out bluntly. Cassio does not disagree, but his response is more decorous:

Iago: … he hath not yet made wanton the night with her, and she is sport for Jove.
Cassio: She's a most exquisite lady.
Iago: And I'll warrant her full of game.
Cassio: Indeed she's a most fresh and delicate creature.

Iago now mentions that he has brought a flagon of wine with him, and has invited a couple of friends to join the two of them. Cassio, uncomfortable with the effects of drink, declines the offer:

Cassio: Not tonight, good Iago, I have very poor and unhappy brains for drinking. I could well wish courtesy would invent some other custom of entertainment.[1]

[1] *I wish that there were some other socially accepted way of showing hospitality*

He reveals that he has already had one drink this evening. Even though it was carefully diluted, he feels the worse for it, and dare not drink any more. However, Iago persuades him to allow his friends to join them.

Cassio leaves, reluctantly, to fetch the men, and while he is gone Iago weighs up the situation. If he can get Cassio to take another drink, he knows that the lieutenant is likely to become moody and aggressive. Iago has already made sure that the other members of Othello's guard have had plenty to drink, including Roderigo, who, infatuated with Desdemona, regards Cassio as his rival. With any luck, Cassio will get himself into trouble:

Iago: … 'mongst this flock of drunkards
Am I to put our Cassio in some action
That may offend this isle.
… If consequence do but approve my dream,[1]
My boat sails freely, both with wind and stream.

[1] *if events turn out as I am hoping*

> *"The cast of characters is small, the atmosphere fevered and claustrophobic ... Most of the action takes place at night, in a darkness sinister in itself which gradually becomes an emblem of the incomprehension, ignorance, and self-delusion of the characters."*
>
> Anne Barton, *Hell and Night*, 1979

A weakness for drink

Cassio returns with Montano and others, complaining that they have encouraged him to drink even more. Iago calls for more wine, and launches into a military drinking-song:

Iago: And let me the cannikin[1] clink, clink,
And let me the cannikin clink.
A soldier's a man,
O, man's life's but a span,[2]
Why then let a soldier drink!

[1] *drinking-can, small tankard*
[2] *a brief period of time*

As the wine flows, and the carousing continues, Cassio quickly becomes befuddled. Eventually, remembering his responsibility as Othello's lieutenant, he leaves the gathering to take up his guard duty. As he staggers away, it is obvious to the others that, despite his protestations, he is drunk:

Cassio: Do not think, gentlemen, I am drunk: this is my ancient,[1] this is my right hand, and this is my left. I am not drunk now: I can stand well enough, and I speak well enough.
Gentlemen: Excellent well.

[1] *Iago*

It is unfortunate, Iago remarks to Montano, that Cassio, who is such a fine soldier, should also be such a heavy drinker. He is worried that the lieutenant's addiction might put Cyprus in danger. Montano is shocked to hear the extent of Cassio's drinking:

Iago: 'Tis pity of him: [1]
I fear the trust Othello puts him in
On some odd time of his infirmity
Will shake this island. [2]
Montano: But is he often thus?
Iago: 'Tis evermore the prologue to his sleep [3] …

[1] *it's a shame about Cassio's flaw*
[2] *his position of responsibility may result in disaster for the island, as he is likely to be incapable if unexpected danger arises*
[3] *he goes to bed drunk every night*

Othello must be told of his lieutenant's weakness, insists Montano. Iago is reluctant. Cassio is his friend, he explains, and he cannot bring himself to do anything that would damage his career. He wishes there were some way of helping him:

Montano: It were an honest action to say so
To the Moor.
Iago: Not I, for this fair island.
I do love Cassio well, and would do much
To cure him of this evil.

Iago briefly leaves his companions to tell Roderigo, waiting nearby, to pursue Cassio. As planned, he is to provoke his rival into a fight.

A breach of the peace

As Iago had predicted, the wine has made Cassio quarrelsome and short-tempered, and he is quickly goaded into an argument. He now runs in, pursuing Roderigo and threatening to attack him.

Montano intervenes and tries to hold Cassio back. Cassio retaliates aggressively, inflicting a severe wound on Montano. As the two of them struggle, Iago takes Roderigo aside and orders him to run out into the crowded streets and start a riot.

An alarm-bell is now rung, adding to the noise and confusion. Finally Othello himself enters, angered by this outbreak of violent disorder:

Othello: Why, how now, ho? From whence ariseth this?
Are we turned Turks? And to ourselves do that
Which heaven hath forbid the Ottomites? [1]
For Christian shame, put by [2] this barbarous brawl;
He that stirs next, to carve for his own rage, [3]
Holds his soul light: he dies upon his motion. [4]
Silence that dreadful bell, it frights the isle …

[1] *commit violence to ourselves where, thanks to a heaven-sent storm, our enemies failed*
[2] *give up, stop*
[3] *to use his sword for his own private disputes*
[4] *the instant that he makes a move*

The general first turns to Iago for an explanation. Iago claims to be utterly mystified: everyone had been behaving perfectly amicably, he claims, until an inexplicable madness swept over them. Othello then questions Cassio, demanding to know why he has neglected his duty so shamefully.

Cassio is unable to answer, and Othello addresses Montano. As the previous governor of the island, he was renowned for his wisdom and his calm disposition: what has possessed him, asks Othello, to take part in this unseemly brawl? Montano, barely able to speak because of his injury, replies that – as Iago can confirm – he was acting in self-defence.

Othello is becoming increasingly impatient. This is a serious matter, he asserts, and he needs to know the truth. The island has narrowly escaped the threat of invasion, and the atmosphere is still tense: this is no time to indulge in private feuds. He turns again to Iago, ordering him to explain how the fighting started. Montano urges him not to be influenced by friendship or loyalty, hinting that he must not excuse Cassio.

Iago makes it clear that he is in a difficult position, and answers with a display of reluctance:

Iago: I had rather have this tongue cut from my mouth
Than it should do offence to Michael Cassio …

He then gives a lengthy explanation confirming that Cassio had indeed drawn his sword first, in pursuit of a stranger who has now vanished. He had then, somehow, become embroiled in a fight with Montano. Cassio's behaviour was entirely out of character, and was no doubt justified by some insult from the stranger, who cannot now be found. Othello is unconvinced:

Iago: … Yet surely Cassio, I believe, received
From him that fled some strange indignity
Which patience could not pass.[1]

Othello: I know, Iago,
Thy honesty and love doth mince[2] this matter,
Making it light[3] to Cassio.

[1] *some offensive comment that could not be tolerated*
[2] *understate, play down*
[3] *less severe*

Othello makes an immediate decision: Cassio is summarily dismissed, and is no longer the general's lieutenant.

> *"'Honest' is the word that springs to the lips of everyone who speaks of Iago. It is applied to him some fifteen times in the play, not to mention some half-dozen where he employs it, in derision, of himself ... If this rough diamond had any flaw, it was that Iago's warm loyal heart incited him to too impulsive action ... such seemed Iago to the people about him, even to those who, like Othello, had known him for some time."*
>
> A. C. Bradley, *Shakespearean Tragedy*, 1904

In disgrace

At this moment Desdemona comes in. The fact that she has been disturbed angers Othello even more, and he vows not to show any mercy to Cassio. He arranges for Montano's wounds to be treated, and instructs Iago to calm down any further disorder in the surrounding streets.

The others leave, and eventually Iago and Cassio are alone. It is clear that Cassio is utterly devastated:

Iago: What, are you hurt, lieutenant?
Cassio: Ay, past all surgery.[1]
Iago: Marry, God forbid!
Cassio: Reputation, reputation, reputation! O, I have lost my reputation, I have lost the immortal part of myself – and what remains is bestial. My reputation, Iago, my reputation!

[1] *beyond the ability of any surgeon to heal me*

Iago bluntly dismisses Cassio's fears. A physical injury might be serious, he says, but it is not worth mourning the loss of something as meaningless as reputation. Othello has punished him merely to demonstrate his authority.

Iago assures Cassio that he will easily win back the general's favour:

Iago: Reputation is an idle and most false imposition, oft got without merit and lost without deserving … You are but now cast in his mood,[1] a punishment more in policy than in malice,[2] even so as one would beat his dog to affright an imperious lion. Sue to him[3] again, and he's yours.

1 *dismissed as a result of an angry fit of temper*
2 *resulting from expedience rather than ill-feeling*
3 *ask him to pardon you*

Cassio, filled with self-loathing, disregards Iago's advice. He is horrified at the effect that the wine has had on him:

Cassio: Drunk? And speak parrot?[1] And squabble? Swagger? Swear? And discourse fustian[2] with one's own shadow? O thou invisible spirit of wine, if thou hast no name to be known by, let us call thee devil!

1 *prattle foolishly*
2 *talk nonsense*

Iago persists. Cassio must stop tormenting himself, he urges, and instead think about practical steps he can take to regain his position as Othello's lieutenant: for example, he could ask Desdemona to plead on his behalf. Her influence over Othello is undoubtedly strong, and she will be more than willing to co-operate:

Iago: I'll tell you what you shall do. Our general's wife is now the general[1] … Confess yourself freely to her, importune her help to put you in your place again. She is of so free, so kind, so apt, so blest a disposition that she holds it a vice in her goodness not to do more than she is requested.

1 *governs her husband*

Cassio's anguish is starting to subside, and he listens to the proposal with interest. He resolves to approach Desdemona tomorrow morning: it is his only hope of recovering his career.

Iago's plan takes shape

Alone, Iago contemplates the development of events. He is amused by the thought that his advice to Cassio is, on the surface, honest and reasonable. After all, Desdemona will be happy to help Cassio, and she certainly has a powerful sway over her husband's emotions.

However, Iago realises that, if he can arouse Othello's jealousy, Desdemona's efforts may have disastrous consequences. In fact, the harder she tries, the more discord she will create:

Iago: … whiles this honest fool
Plies Desdemona to repair his fortune,
And she for him pleads strongly to the Moor,
I'll pour this pestilence into his ear:
That she repeals him[1] for her body's lust.
And by how much she strives to do him good
She shall undo her credit with the Moor –
So will I turn her virtue into pitch[2]
And out of her own goodness make the net
That shall enmesh[3] them all.

1 *pleads for his reinstatement*
2 *black, sticky tar*
3 *trap, entangle*

Roderigo now comes to confront Iago. He is thoroughly dejected by the current state of affairs. The clash with Cassio has left him in pain, his hopes of winning Desdemona's love are fading, and he has gained nothing of value from his expedition to Cyprus:

Roderigo: My money is almost spent, I have been tonight exceedingly well cudgelled,[1] and I think the issue will be I shall have so much experience for my pains:[2] and so, with no money at all, and a little more wit,[3] return again to Venice.

1 *beaten*
2 *my profit will be nothing but the experience itself*
3 *wisdom*

Iago urges Roderigo to be patient. His rival Cassio has been dismissed, he points out, so he is one step closer to achieving his goal. Promising him that there will soon be further good news, he hurries the young man away.

The new day is dawning, and Iago, now full of energy, considers what must be done next. First he will instruct his wife, who is Desdemona's maidservant, to mention Cassio's predicament to her mistress. Later, when Cassio visits Desdemona to plead his case, Iago will ensure that Othello is there to observe their meeting. There is no time to lose:

Iago: … draw the Moor apart [1]
And bring him jump [2] when he may Cassio find
Soliciting his wife: ay, that's the way!
Dull not device [3] by coldness and delay!

[1] *take Othello aside*
[2] *precisely, at exactly the right time and place*
[3] *don't let the scheme lose its energy*

Cassio's wish is granted III, i

Cassio has hired a group of musicians to play outside Othello's lodgings, as an early morning greeting to the general and his new wife. An eccentric servant sent down by Othello makes it clear that the music is not entirely welcome:

Clown: … masters, here's money for you, and the general so likes your music that he desires you, for love's sake, to make no more noise with it.
Musician: Well, sir, we will not.
Clown: If you have any music that may not be heard, to't again.[1] But, as they say, to hear music the general does not greatly care.
Musician: We have none such, sir.

[1] *go ahead, carry on playing*

The musicians leave. Just as the servant is about to return indoors, Cassio stops him and, handing him a gold coin, asks for a word with Desdemona's maidservant Emilia. At this moment, Iago appears: when he hears that Cassio wants to talk to his wife Emilia, he offers to go into Othello's quarters himself to find her. Cassio accepts gratefully, and as Iago leaves he reflects on the ancient's helpful, reliable nature.

Emilia soon emerges. She sympathises with Cassio's plight, and assures him that Desdemona has already raised the matter with Othello. The general had no choice but to dismiss Cassio, she explains, because of the great popularity and reputation of Montano, the man he injured in the brawl. However, she is confident that in the fullness of time Cassio will find favour with Othello once more:

Emilia: ... he protests he loves you
And needs no other suitor but his likings [1]
To take the safest occasion by the front [2]
To bring you in again.

[1] *needs no request, as his own feelings are in your favour*
[2] *to seize the opportunity when the time is right*

Cassio, however, still feels that he needs to speak to Desdemona in person. To his relief and gratitude, Emilia agrees to arrange a private meeting with her straight away, and the two of them go inside.

"As only the audience and none of the actors except Iago know the extent of his machinations, a kind of complicity has developed between them ... All the characters except Iago are hoodwinked by darkness."

Germaine Greer, *Shakespeare*, 1986

Desdemona speaks her mind III, ii – iii

Iago is escorting Othello as he goes about his duties. The general gives him some letters to be despatched to Venice: when he has given them to the ship's captain, he is to join Othello on an inspection of the island's fortifications.

Meanwhile, Cassio is with Desdemona. She reassures him, as Emilia did earlier, that he will soon be reinstated as Othello's lieutenant. For the sake of appearances, her husband must remain aloof from Cassio for the time being, but the relationship between them will soon be as cordial as it was before.

Cassio is grateful, but is concerned that the general will quickly become used to the present situation, particularly if a new lieutenant is appointed. He fears that, in time, he will simply be forgotten, and his years of faithful service will count for nothing. Desdemona promises that she will not allow this to happen, and urges him not to worry:

Desdemona: My lord shall never rest,
I'll watch him tame[1] and talk him out of patience,
His bed shall seem a school,[2] his board a shrift,[3]
I'll intermingle everything he does
With Cassio's suit:[4] therefore be merry, Cassio …

[1] *keep him awake until I wear down his resistance*
[2] *even in bed he will feel as if he is being lectured*
[3] *every mealtime will be like a confessional*
[4] *appeal, petition*

Othello now returns, accompanied by Iago. Desdemona is happy for Cassio to stay while she talks to her husband, but Cassio, uneasy about being in Othello's presence, makes a hasty exit.

Iago subtly draws Othello's attention to the fact that a man has suddenly left his wife's company, hinting that something suspicious may be going on. He starts with an offhand comment, supposedly to himself, but designed to be overheard by Othello:

Iago: Ha, I like not that.[1]
Othello: What dost thou say?
Iago: Nothing, my lord: or if – I know not what.
Othello: Was not that Cassio parted from my wife?
Iago: Cassio, my lord? No, sure, I cannot think it
That he would steal away so guilty-like
Seeing you coming.

[1] *I don't like the look of that*

Desdemona comes to meet her husband, and immediately appeals to him, as she had promised, on Cassio's behalf. Othello is taken aback to discover that it had indeed been Cassio who was with her, but he listens patiently as she calls for the lieutenant to be restored to his position as soon as possible.

It is understandable, says Desdemona, that Cassio, as a soldier, had to be punished; on the other hand, his crime was relatively minor. She mentions that Cassio helped to bring them together, and often spoke up for Othello when she was critical of him:

Desdemona: What, Michael Cassio
That came a-wooing with you? And so many a time
When I have spoke of you dispraisingly
Hath ta'en your part[1] …

[1] *taken your side, spoken in your favour*

Othello finally agrees. He cannot refuse her anything, he admits, and Cassio can return to his post as soon as he wishes. Desdemona points out that he should not bring Cassio back as a favour to her, but because it is the right course of action.

Repeating that he can deny her nothing, Othello asks her, in return, to leave him on his own for a while. She will always obey him, she replies, whatever his feelings may dictate. When she has left, Othello reveals how deeply he loves her:

Othello: Excellent wretch! Perdition catch my soul
But I do love thee! [1] And when I love thee not
Chaos is come again. [2]

[1] *may my soul be damned if I don't love you*
[2] *the world will return to its primeval state of disorder*

Seeds of doubt

With a show of hesitancy, Iago now raises the subject of Cassio's role in the courtship of Othello and Desdemona. He claims to be surprised that Cassio was involved in helping them.

Othello is perplexed by Iago's apparent uneasiness in discussing the subject, and eventually becomes exasperated:

Iago: I did not think he had been acquainted with her.
Othello: O yes, and went between us very oft.
Iago: Indeed?
Othello: Indeed? Ay, indeed. Discern'st thou aught [1] in that?
Is he not honest?
Iago: Honest, my lord?
Othello: Honest? Ay, honest.
Iago: My lord, for aught I know. [2]
Othello: What dost thou think?
Iago: Think, my lord?
Othello: Think, my lord! By heaven, thou echo'st me
As if there were some monster in thy thought
Too hideous to be shown …

[1] *do you see anything strange*
[2] *as far as I know*

Othello considers Iago to be an honest and loyal companion, and one who chooses his words carefully. He is all the more alarmed by Iago's awkwardness: he is clearly hiding something, and Othello demands to know what is on his mind.

Iago appears to emphasise Cassio's honesty while continuing, slowly but surely, to raise Othello's suspicions:

Iago: For Michael Cassio,
I dare be sworn, I think, that he is honest.
Othello: I think so too.
Iago: Men should be what they seem,
Or those that be not, would they might seem none.[1]
Othello: Certain, men should be what they seem.
Iago: Why then I think Cassio's an honest man.
Othello: Nay, yet there's more in this …

[1] *as for those who are not honest, it would be preferable if they did not act as if they were*

By now Othello is desperate to know exactly what Iago is keeping from him. Iago complains that some thoughts are best kept private; after all, he points out, no-one is entirely innocent.

Othello is adamant, but Iago insists on keeping his suspicions to himself. His concerns may be misguided, and besides, he would be loath to harm anyone's reputation:

Iago: Good name in man and woman, dear my lord,
Is the immediate jewel of their souls:
Who steals my purse steals trash – 'tis something, nothing,
'Twas mine, 'tis his, and has been slave to thousands –
But he that filches from me my good name
Robs me of that which not enriches him
And makes me poor indeed.
Othello: By heaven, I'll know thy thoughts!

Iago still refuses to say what it is that he suspects, and warns Othello against pursuing these worries and questions. Living in a constant state of doubt is intolerable, he tells him, giving the example of a man who distrusts his wife as opposed to one who knows her to be unfaithful:

Iago: O beware, my lord, of jealousy!
It is the green-eyed monster, which doth mock
The meat it feeds on. That cuckold [1] lives in bliss
Who, certain of his fate, loves not his wronger,[2]
But O, what damned minutes tells he o'er [3]
Who dotes yet doubts, suspects yet strongly loves!
Othello: O misery!

[1] *husband whose wife is unfaithful*
[2] *the wife who wrongs him*
[3] *he counts, one by one*

"To anyone capable of reading the play with an open mind as to its merits, it is obvious that Shakespear plunged through it so impetuously that he had it finished before he had made up his mind as to the character and motives of a single person in it ... It remains magnificent by the volume of its passion and the splendour of its word-music, which sweep across the scenes up to a plane on which sense is drowned in sound ... The actor cannot help himself by studying his part acutely; for there is nothing to study in it. Tested by the brain, it is ridiculous: tested by the ear, it is sublime."

George Bernard Shaw, *Mainly About Shakespear*, 1897

Othello is tormented

At this point Othello's tone suddenly changes, and he shakes off his mood of despair. He refuses to be plagued by the jealousy that Iago describes. Desdemona is beautiful, sociable, sincere, and talented; but none of this means that she is untrustworthy. If there were genuine cause for doubting Desdemona, and he saw the evidence with his own eyes, he would cast her off without further ado. As things are, however, he is confident of her loyalty.

Iago too changes his tone. He welcomes Othello's more pragmatic attitude, he claims, because he too can now speak more frankly. He agrees that evidence is what they need, and he advises Othello to watch his wife with an impartial eye. He will need to be attentive, warns Iago; Venetian women are notorious for their secretive affairs. Othello is shaken:

Iago: I speak not yet of proof:
Look to your wife, observe her well with Cassio.
Wear your eyes thus, not jealous nor secure …
I know our country disposition[1] well –
In Venice they do let God see the pranks
They dare not show their husbands; their best
conscience[2]
Is not to leave't undone, but keep't unknown.
Othello: Dost thou say so?

[1] *the character of the Venetians*
[2] *what they aspire to, their ideal*

Iago then points out that she has already deceived her father with their secret elopement; indeed, she has in a sense deceived Othello himself, appearing at first to be overawed by him and his experiences when in reality she loved him. Othello agrees, his earlier resolve giving way to dejection.

Observing Othello's mood, Iago apologises. It is his love for the general that has persuaded him to be so blunt; besides, these suspicions may be entirely unfounded. Othello denies that he is upset, and Iago assures him, unconvincingly, that both Cassio and Desdemona may be blameless:

Iago: … Cassio's my worthy friend.
My lord, I see you're moved.
Othello: No, not much moved.
I do not think but[1] Desdemona's honest.
Iago: Long live she so; and long live you to think so.

[1] *I'm sure it is true that*

Aware of Othello's vulnerability, Iago continues to torment him, carefully tempering his wounding comments with apologies. He mentions that Desdemona has turned down offers of marriage from those of her own nationality, race and social standing, going completely against custom, even against nature:

Iago: … one may smell in such[1] a will most rank,[2]
Foul disproportion,[3] thoughts unnatural.
But pardon me, I do not in position
Distinctly speak of her[4] …

[1] *suspect in such a person*
[2] *an uncontrolled, lustful appetite*
[3] *impropriety*
[4] *in suggesting these things, I'm not talking specifically about Desdemona*

Othello asks his companion to leave him with his thoughts. He is convinced, in his anguish, that Iago is still not revealing everything he knows about Desdemona.

Just before leaving, Iago suggests to Othello that he should delay his reinstatement of Cassio for a while to see what happens. If Desdemona continues to press for his return, it will be a sure sign that something is amiss. All the same, he assures Othello, there may be nothing to be concerned about: and with a final appeal not to think ill of Desdemona, Iago takes his leave.

A lucky find

Alone, Othello reflects on the overwhelming anxiety now lodged in his mind. He is convinced that Iago has a profound understanding of human nature, and his suspicions cannot be ignored.

Othello eventually persuades himself that the only course of action that will resolve the situation is to reject Desdemona. She has never loved him, and his short-lived marriage is over:

Othello: Haply for[1] I am black
And have not those soft parts of conversation
That chamberers[2] have, or for I am declined
Into the vale of years[3] – yet that's not much –
She's gone. I am abused,[4] and my relief
Must be to loathe her. O curse of marriage
That we can call these delicate creatures ours
And not their appetites!

[1] *perhaps because*
[2] *do not have the refined manners of a courtier*
[3] *descending into the valley of old age*
[4] *wronged, deceived*

He is still in turmoil, however, and when Desdemona appears his feelings change instantly:

Othello: Look where she comes:
If she be false, O then heaven mocks itself,
I'll not believe't.

Desdemona reminds Othello that they are holding a banquet for the nobility of Cyprus, and their guests are waiting. He apologises, and it is immediately clear to Desdemona that her husband is troubled. When questioned, he claims to have a headache, and she offers to bind his forehead with her handkerchief. He brushes it away impatiently, and they leave to greet his guests.

Desdemona's maidservant Emilia notices the dropped handkerchief and picks it up. Iago has often asked her to steal it for him, she remarks, though she has no idea why. She has always refused, knowing that it is very special to Desdemona, as it was Othello's first gift to her. She decides to have a copy made for Iago before she returns it to her mistress.

Iago now enters. When he learns that his wife has obtained the handkerchief, he snatches it from her impatiently, ignoring her protests. If Desdemona asks about the handkerchief, he tells her bluntly, she should claim to know nothing about it.

Ordering Emilia away, Iago contemplates the handkerchief with relish. If he can arrange for it to be discovered in Cassio's lodgings, Othello's jealousy will be inflamed even further. Othello himself now approaches, and as Iago puts the handkerchief away, he remarks that he has already succeeded in changing the Moor's life for ever:

Iago: Not poppy nor mandragora [1]
Nor all the drowsy syrups of the world
Shall ever medicine thee to that sweet sleep
Which thou owedst [2] yesterday.

[1] *root of the mandrake plant, a powerful sedative*
[2] *possessed, enjoyed*

"In his motives, his judgements, and his single-minded savagery, Iago embodies his victim's psychological flaws. Iago can triumph only because Othello rejects his own potential for love and trust in favour of the self-centred desperation of jealousy and envy, the passions that dominate Iago."

Charles Boyce, *Shakespeare A to Z*, 1990

Othello demands proof

Iago is startled to find that his attempts to arouse Othello's jealousy have been even more effective than he had imagined. It is clear at once that the general's emotional turmoil has driven him to the verge of madness. He launches into a violent outburst, blaming Iago for revealing his wife's infidelity and poisoning his mind:

Othello: Avaunt,[1] be gone, thou hast set me on the rack!
I swear 'tis better to be much abused
Than but to know't a little.[2]
Iago: How now, my lord?
Othello: What sense[3] had I of her stolen hours of lust?
I saw't not, thought it not, it harmed not me,
I slept the next night well, fed well, was free and merry;
I found not Cassio's kisses on her lips …

1 *away, out of my sight*
2 *it's better to be completely deceived than to know only a little of what has happened*
3 *awareness, knowledge*

In Othello's tortured imagination, he sees the end of his happiness and the destruction of his whole career, brought about by the terrible knowledge of Desdemona's debauchery:

Othello: I had been happy if the general camp,
Pioneers and all,[1] had tasted her sweet body,
So[2] I had nothing known. O now for ever
Farewell the tranquil mind, farewell content!
… Farewell the neighing steed and the shrill trump,
The spirit-stirring drum, th'ear-piercing fife,[3]
The royal banner, and all quality,[4]
Pride, pomp and circumstance of glorious war!

1 *the whole army, including the lowest-ranked soldiers*
2 *as long as*
3 *military flute, pipe*
4 *nature, character*

Becoming increasingly agitated, Othello grabs hold of Iago. He must have proof, he declares. If Iago cannot demonstrate, beyond doubt, that Desdemona is unfaithful, his punishment will be more horrific than he can imagine.

Iago responds by vowing never again to be honest; telling the truth to a friend, apparently, leads to trouble. His love for Othello, he complains, has only brought him abuse. At this, Othello relents and calms down a little, but he remains bewildered by his turbulent feelings.

Playing on Othello's worst fears, Iago now comes back to the practicalities of finding evidence. He suggests that observing Desdemona and Cassio during their lovemaking might not be a realistic possibility:

Iago: I see, sir, you are eaten up with passion.
I do repent me that I put it to you.
You would[1] be satisfied?
Othello: Would? Nay, and I will!
Iago: And may – but how? How satisfied, my lord?
Would you, the supervisor,[2] grossly gape on?
Behold her topped?[3]
Othello: Death and damnation!

[1] *wish to*
[2] *spectator, onlooker*
[3] *mated, copulated with (referring to animals)*

Iago promises that he can provide a wealth of circumstantial evidence, however. Insisting that he is unwilling to talk of these matters, he describes a recent episode when he was sharing a room with Cassio. Unable to sleep, he was shocked at his friend's night-time revelations:

Iago: In sleep I heard him say 'Sweet Desdemona,
Let us be wary, let us hide our loves,'
And then, sir, would he gripe[1] and wring my hand,
Cry 'O sweet creature!' and then kiss me hard
As if he plucked up kisses by the roots
That grew upon my lips …

[1] *grasp*

Solemn vows

Othello's grief and revulsion are now turning to violent anger. Iago assures the general yet again that his wife may be innocent. He chooses this moment to mention, casually, another piece of evidence:

Iago: Nay, yet be wise, yet we see nothing done,
She may be honest yet. Tell me but this,
Have you not sometimes seen a handkerchief
Spotted with strawberries, in your wife's hand?
Othello: I gave her such a one, 'twas my first gift.
Iago: I know not that, but such a handkerchief,
I am sure it was your wife's, did I today
See Cassio wipe his beard with.

Othello's anger now boils over. There is no longer the slightest doubt in his mind. Cassio must die:

Othello: O that the slave had forty thousand lives!
One is too poor, too weak for my revenge.
Now do I see 'tis true.

Kneeling to take his oath, Othello makes a sacred vow that he will take revenge. Nothing now will change his mind. Seeing his master kneel, Iago does the same, and he too gives his word:

Iago: … Witness that here Iago doth give up
The execution[1] of his wit,[2] hands, heart,
To wronged Othello's service. Let him command
And to obey shall be in me remorse
What bloody business ever.[3]

[1] *use, performance*
[2] *mind*
[3] *in my compassion for my master I shall carry out whatever brutal actions he commands*

Iago's vow will be put to the test immediately, Othello tells him:

Othello: Within these three days let me hear thee say
That Cassio's not alive.

Iago agrees without hesitation. He then raises the question of Desdemona. She too must die, decides Othello. The course of action resolved, Othello finally utters the words that Iago has long waited to hear:

Iago: My friend is dead,
'Tis done – at your request. But let her live.
Othello: Damn her, lewd minx: O damn her, damn her!
Come, go with me apart;[1] I will withdraw
To furnish me with some swift means of death
For the fair devil. Now art thou my lieutenant.
Iago: I am your own for ever.

[1] *away from here, to a private location*

... some swift means of death
For the fair devil.

"Desdemona is trapped in the definition of 'fair devil', since even her faithful conformity to traditional feminine virtues of modesty and submission is read as a mark of deception."

Alison Findlay, *Women in Shakespeare*, 2014

A bitter dispute

III, iv

Desdemona, unaware of what has passed between Iago and Othello, wishes to contact Cassio with some good news: since their last meeting, she has successfully persuaded her husband to reinstate him as the general's lieutenant. She intends to send for him, but first needs to know where his lodgings are.

Her servant, after admitting that he does not know, promises in his verbose manner to find Cassio and pass on the message:

Clown: I will catechize the world for him, that is, make questions and by them answer.
Desdemona: Seek him, bid him come hither, tell him I have moved my lord on his behalf, and hope all will be well.
Clown: To do this is within the compass of man's wit, and therefore I will attempt the doing of it.

Desdemona mentions the loss of her precious handkerchief, but Emilia claims that she has not seen it. Although the loss is upsetting, Desdemona is grateful that her husband is not the kind of man to be suspicious of such an incident:

Emilia: Is he not jealous?
Desdemona: Who, he? I think the sun where he was born
Drew all such humours[1] from him.

[1] *removed all qualities of that kind*

Othello himself now appears. Controlling his feelings with difficulty, he takes Desdemona's hand. His comments are ambiguous, superficially light-hearted but full of significance:

Othello: Give me your hand. This hand is moist, my lady.
Desdemona: It yet hath felt no age, nor known no sorrow.
Othello: This argues [1] fruitfulness and liberal heart:
Hot, hot and moist …
… 'Tis a good hand,
A frank one.
Desdemona: You may indeed say so,
For 'twas that hand that gave away my heart.

[1] *suggests, indicates*

Desdemona, determined to settle the matter of Cassio's position, mentions that he will shortly be joining them. Othello, keeping his emotions under control, remarks that he has a cold that is troubling him; he needs a handkerchief.

The handkerchief that Desdemona hands him is not the strawberry-patterned one that he once gave her as a love-token. Othello's tone now becomes more sinister as he questions her about it. Desdemona claims that she has not lost the handkerchief, merely mislaid it temporarily. She is shocked when Othello describes its importance:

Othello: That handkerchief
Did an Egyptian to my mother give;
She was a charmer [1] and could almost read
The thoughts of people. She told her, while she kept it
'Twould make her amiable and subdue my father
Entirely to her love …
To lose't or give't away were such perdition [2]
As nothing else could match.
Desdemona: Is't possible?
Othello: 'Tis true, there's magic in the web [3] of it.

[1] *sorceress, witch*
[2] *loss; damnation*
[3] *weave, texture*

Othello, becoming angry, again demands to see it, and Desdemona again claims that she has not lost it. She tries to talk instead about Cassio's appeal, but Othello is adamant:

Othello: Fetch't, let me see't.
Desdemona: Why, so I can, sir; but I will not now.
This is a trick to put me from my suit.[1]
Pray you, let Cassio be received again.
Othello: Fetch me the handkerchief, my mind misgives.[2]

[1] *to distract me from my request*
[2] *is apprehensive, full of doubt*

The argument builds to a crescendo, Othello demanding to see the handkerchief and Desdemona trying to argue Cassio's case. Finally, with a cry of rage, Othello storms out.

Desdemona is unsure

The quarrel leaves Desdemona stunned; she has never seen Othello so angry. Emilia comments, cynically, that all men eventually show their true colours; and despite Desdemona's earlier claim, he does indeed seem to have a jealous nature.

Cassio now arrives, accompanied by Iago. He explains again how eager he is to return to Othello's service. If this is impossible, he will resign himself to seeking some other occupation, but he urgently needs an answer.

Desdemona apologises; she has spoken in Cassio's favour, but her husband is in a strange, unsettled mood at the moment. This news catches Iago's attention. The general is rarely angry, he says, even in the midst of war, and he leaves in search of Othello.

By now, Desdemona is starting to feel more positive. She is sure that his ill temper relates to important affairs of state, and that he has directed his anger instead into more trivial matters. She is ashamed of herself, she tells Emilia, for setting her standards so high; Othello is only human, after all.

Emilia replies that they must hope for the best:

Emilia: Pray heaven it be
State matters, as you think, and no conception
Nor no jealous toy,[1] concerning you.
Desdemona: Alas the day, I never gave him cause.

[1] *no misguided notion or irrational jealous idea*

Jealousy does not need a cause, maintains Emilia. It provides its own motivation:

Emilia: But jealous souls will not be answered so:
They are not ever jealous for the cause,
But jealous for[1] they're jealous. It is a monster
Begot upon itself, born on itself.

[1] *because*

Emilia's words make Desdemona uneasy, and she decides to find Othello and talk to him again.

Cassio's sweetheart

As Cassio waits for Desdemona and Othello to return, his lover Bianca appears. He has not visited her for a week now, and she chides him for his absence. He has had a lot on his mind, he explains, promising to devote more time to her as soon as he can.

Cassio then asks Bianca a favour. He shows her a handkerchief; he would like her to make a copy of it. Bianca is offended. The beautifully patterned handkerchief is clearly a gift from another woman, and his request is adding insult to injury:

Bianca: O Cassio, whence came this?
This is some token from a newer friend!
To the felt absence now I feel a cause:[1]
Is't come to this?

[1] *on top of the pain of your absence, I'm suffering even more because I know the reason for it*

There is no reason to be jealous, Cassio assures her. He found the handkerchief in his lodgings, he claims; how it came to be there is a mystery. The owner will undoubtedly want it back eventually, and Cassio would like a copy made before he has to return it.

Cassio then urges Bianca to leave him. He is expecting to meet Othello shortly, and would rather be on his own. Bianca, still displeased, insists that he must at least walk a little way home with her, and Cassio reluctantly agrees.

Bianca is generally described as a 'courtesan', a prostitute whose clients were typically wealthy and influential. The figure of the courtesan was strongly associated with Venice in Shakespeare's day; the republic's status as a major political, commercial and naval power was matched by its reputation for hedonism and sexual freedom. An English travel writer of the time expressed a combination of disapproval and fascination:

"As for the number of these Venetian courtesans, it is very great. For it is thought there are of them in the whole city and other adjacent places at the least twenty thousand ... A most ungodly thing without doubt that there should be a toleration of such licentious wantons in so glorious, so potent, so renowned a city ... The revenues which they pay unto the Senate for their toleration do maintain a dozen of their galleys, as many reported unto me in Venice ... I will tell thee this news which is most true, that if thou shouldst wantonly converse with her and not give her that salarium iniquitatis[1] *which thou hast promised her but perhaps cunningly escape from her company, she will either cause thy throat to be cut by her* ruffiano[2] *if he can after catch thee in the city, or procure thee to be arrested if thou art to be found, and clapped up in the prison ..."*

[1] *wages of sin; payment*
[2] *pimp*

Thomas Coryate, *Coryate's Crudities*, 1611

Iago takes control

IV, i

Othello and Iago are deep in conversation. Othello's attention is captivated by Iago's ambiguous, provocative comments:

Iago: … if I give my wife a handkerchief –
Othello: What then?
Iago: Why, then 'tis hers, my lord, and being hers
She may, I think, bestow't on any man.
Othello: She is protectress of her honour too:
May she give that?
Iago: Her honour is an essence that's not seen,
They have it very oft that have it not.[1]

[1] *those who are credited with honour are often without it*

Iago now goes as far as to suggest that he has heard Cassio bragging of his sexual conquest of Desdemona. Othello is horrified but enthralled:

Othello: Hath he said anything?
Iago: He hath, my lord, but be you well assured
No more than he'll unswear.[1]
Othello: What hath he said?
Iago: Faith, that he did – I know not what. He did –
Othello: What? What?
Iago: Lie.
Othello: With her?
Iago: With her, on her, what you will.

[1] *believe me, he'll deny everything that he has said*

Overwhelmed with jealousy, and tormented by the image of Desdemona's handkerchief, Othello gives way to an incoherent fit of rage. Eventually he falls, semi-conscious, to the ground. Iago revels in his success:

Iago: Work on,
My medicine, work! Thus credulous fools are caught …

At this point Cassio approaches. Iago urges him not to disturb the general; this is his second fit in two days, he reveals, and the best thing to do is to let him recover gradually. He asks Cassio to leave them for the moment, but to return soon as there is a very important matter he wishes to discuss.

As Othello regains consciousness, it is clear that he is still reflecting obsessively on Cassio and Desdemona. Iago assures him briskly that he is not the only husband betrayed in this way:

Othello: Did he confess it?
Iago: Good sir, be a man,
Think every bearded fellow that's but yoked [1]
May draw with you. [2] There's millions now alive
That nightly lie in those unproper beds [3]
Which they dare swear peculiar [4] …

[1] *harnessed; married*
[2] *carry the same burden of betrayal as you*
[3] *beds that are not exclusively their own*
[4] *restricted to themselves*

Iago now instructs Othello to move to a nearby spot where he can witness what is about to happen. Cassio is soon to come this way, and Iago promises that every last intimate detail of the young man's affair with Desdemona will be revealed:

Iago: Do but encave [1] yourself
And mark the fleers, the gibes and notable scorns [2]
That dwell in every region of his face;
For I will make him tell the tale anew
Where, how, how oft, how long ago, and when
He hath and is again to cope [3] your wife.

[1] *conceal*
[2] *the sneers, jokes and mockery*
[3] *copulate with*

It is essential that Othello remains calm and quiet in his hiding-place. It would not be manly, warns Iago, to give in to the temptation to confront Cassio. Othello agrees:

Othello: Dost thou hear, Iago?
I will be found most cunning in my patience
But – dost thou hear? – most bloody.

An eavesdropper

Iago's plan is to question Cassio not about Desdemona but about his lover Bianca. He knows that she is devoted to Cassio; and while Cassio is fond of her, he finds her excessive displays of affection amusing and, at times, trying. If they talk mockingly about Bianca, Iago hopes to trick Othello into believing that Desdemona is the subject of their conversation. Othello will, at last, have the proof that he has been demanding.

Cassio now returns, as arranged. On greeting him, Iago comments ambiguously on his relationship with Desdemona:

Iago: How do you now, lieutenant?
Cassio: The worser, that you give me the addition
Whose want even kills me.[1]
Iago: Ply[2] Desdemona well, and you are sure on't.[3]

[1] *the lack of the title that you attribute to me (lieutenant) is causing me deadly pain*
[2] *work on, persuade*
[3] *you'll get what you want*

Speaking more quietly for a moment so that Othello will not overhear, Iago mentions that Cassio's plight would be much easier if the decision were up to Bianca.

Cassio laughs out loud at the mention of Bianca, and Iago continues to tease him about their relationship. There is a rumour that he intends to marry her, claims Iago, an idea that Cassio finds hilarious; she is hardly any better than a common prostitute, he retorts.

Othello, watching and listening intently from his hiding-place, is burning with jealousy. He is determined to have his revenge:

Iago:	She gives it out that you shall marry her; Do you intend it?
Cassio:	… I marry! What, a customer! Prithee bear some charity to my wit,[1] do not think it so unwholesome. Ha, ha, ha!
Othello:	So, so, so, so: they laugh that win.[2]
Iago:	Faith, the cry[3] goes that you shall marry her.

[1] *don't insult my intelligence*
[2] *the winner will have the last laugh*
[3] *rumour, gossip*

Cassio denies starting such a rumour; it must have come from the girl herself, who adores him. She never leaves him alone, he complains, and only the other day she embarrassed him with a public display of affection. In fact, the time has probably come to bring the relationship to an end.

To the men's surprise, Bianca herself now appears. She has had second thoughts about copying the handkerchief for Cassio. She is certain that he is lying about finding it in his room, and she flings it back at him furiously:

Bianca:	Let the devil and his dam haunt you! What did you mean by that same handkerchief you gave me even now? … This is some minx's token, and I must take out the work?[1] There, give it your hobby-horse;[2] wheresoever you had it, I'll take out no work on't!

[1] *make a copy of it*
[2] *whore*

She storms away. Cassio, worried that she will start denouncing him in public, pursues her.

The final decision

Othello now emerges from his hiding-place. Cassio's death is beyond question, but Othello is still torn by his feelings for Desdemona. Any such emotions must be suppressed immediately, insists Iago:

Othello: O, the world hath not a sweeter creature: she might lie by an emperor's side and command him tasks.
Iago: Nay, that's not your way.
Othello: Hang her, I do but say what she is: so delicate with her needle, an admirable musician. O, she will sing the savageness out of a bear! Of so high and plenteous wit and invention! [1]
Iago: She's the worse for all this.
Othello: O, a thousand, a thousand times: and then of so gentle a condition.
Iago: Ay, too gentle.[2]
Othello: Nay, that's certain. But yet the pity of it, Iago – O, Iago, the pity of it, Iago!

1 *intelligence and imagination*
2 *too compliant*

Eventually Othello is convinced: Desdemona too must die. He accepts Iago's decision on the means of death:

Othello: Get me some poison, Iago, this night. I'll not expostulate [1] with her, lest her body and beauty unprovide my mind [2] again. This night, Iago.
Iago: Do it not with poison, strangle her in her bed – even the bed she hath contaminated.
Othello: Good, good, the justice of it pleases; very good!
Iago: And for Cassio, let me be his undertaker.

1 *reason, argue*
2 *disarm me, win me over*

What drives Iago in his quest to destroy Othello and those around him? The question of Iago's motivation has long been a subject of discussion and disagreement among critics.

"Shakespeare assigns motives enough; the difficulty is that he assigns so many ... These motives appear and disappear in the most extraordinary manner ... Iago's longing to satisfy the sense of power is the strongest of the forces that drive him on."

A. C. Bradley, *Shakespearean Tragedy*, 1904

"... it is plain that what we should see in Iago's prompt success is not so much Iago's diabolic intellect as Othello's readiness to respond ... the essential traitor is within the gates."

F. R. Leavis, *Diabolic Intellect and the Noble Hero*, 1937

"What Shakespeare gives us in Iago is a portrait of a practical joker of a peculiarly appalling kind ..."

W. H. Auden, *The Dyer's Hand*, 1962

"Iago hates first, and only then seems to invent reasons for his hate ... Thwarted ambition, jealousy of his wife, of Desdemona, of all women and all men: his hate constantly looks for nourishment to feed itself on and is never satisfied."

Jan Kott, *Shakespeare Our Contemporary*, 1964

"... Iago is a failed human being. He is full of self-loathing. The real jealousy at work in the play is not Othello's, but Iago's. When he speaks of jealousy as a green-eyed monster Iago knows what he is talking about. He's been there."

Ben Okri, *A Way of Being Free*, 1997

"Iago differs from his fellow Venetians only in the ferocity with which he espouses their values and the deadly extremes to which he resorts to vindicate them. His devious stratagem works so well because it works by reflecting his victims' own beliefs ..."

Kiernan Ryan, *Racism, misogyny and 'motiveless malignity' in* Othello, 2016

A message from Venice

A trumpet sounds. Lodovico, a Venetian nobleman, has just arrived with a letter from the Duke and senators of Venice. Othello, after greeting the visitor, goes aside to read the contents. However, he cannot restrain himself from crying out when he overhears Desdemona:

Lodovico: Is there division[1] 'twixt my lord and Cassio?
Desdemona: A most unhappy one: I would do much
T'atone[2] them, for the love I bear to Cassio.
Othello: Fire and brimstone!
Desdemona: My lord?
Othello: Are you wise?
Desdemona: What, is he angry?
Lodovico: Maybe the letter moved him.
For, as I think, they do command him home,
Deputing Cassio in his government.[3]

[1] *disagreement, discord*
[2] *to reconcile*
[3] *appointing Cassio as governor of Cyprus*

Desdemona is relieved to hear that she and Othello will be returning to Venice. Othello, becoming increasingly agitated, now approaches Desdemona and strikes her violently. Lodovico is appalled:

Lodovico: My lord, this would not be believed in Venice
Though[1] I should swear I saw't. 'Tis very much;
Make her amends, she weeps.
Othello: O devil, devil!
If that the earth could teem with[2] woman's tears
Each drop she falls would prove a crocodile:[3]
Out of my sight!

[1] *even if*
[2] *could be made fertile by*
[3] *each tear of Desdemona's would produce a crocodile (a creature whose tears were believed to be false)*

Desdemona leaves, bewildered by her husband's behaviour. Othello comments sarcastically on her obedience; she will obey any man, he suggests. He attempts to address his visitors rationally, but can barely contain his chaotic emotions, and he too leaves.

Lodovico is dismayed at the change that has come over the general once famed for his dignity and stoicism. Iago implies that Othello is becoming mentally unstable:

Lodovico: Is this the noble Moor whom our full senate
Call all in all sufficient? [1] This the nature
Whom passion could not shake? …
Iago: He is much changed.
Lodovico: Are his wits safe? Is he not light of brain?
Iago: He's that [2] he is: I may not breathe my censure
What he might be; [3] if what he might, he is not,
I would to heaven he were! [4]

[1] *capable in every way*
[2] *what*
[3] *I had better not give my judgement as to what he may have become*
[4] *if he is not mentally deranged, I wish he were, as that would at least excuse his behaviour*

This is not the only time that Othello has behaved violently towards his wife, Iago hints to Lodovico. However, discretion prevents him from saying any more:

Iago: Alas, alas!
It is not honesty in me to speak
What I have seen and known.

Othello's verdict

Othello is questioning Emilia closely about her mistress. She has never seen anything suspicious in Desdemona's behaviour, she insists, and expresses a heartfelt plea for Othello to abandon his jealous fears. He instructs her to bring Desdemona to him, and it becomes clear that he is not convinced by the maidservant's words:

Emilia: I durst, my lord, to wager she is honest,
Lay down my soul at stake:[1] if you think other
Remove your thought, it doth abuse your bosom.
If any wretch have put this in your head
Let heaven requite it with the serpent's curse[2] …
Othello: Bid her come hither; go. [*Emilia leaves*]
She says enough; yet she's a simple bawd
That cannot say as much.[3] This[4] is a subtle whore …

[1] *I would dare to gamble my soul on the fact that she is virtuous*
[2] *may heaven take vengeance, just as it did against the serpent that tempted Eve*
[3] *Emilia's words are plausible, but she's a simple go-between who has been told what to say*
[4] *Desdemona*

Emilia now returns with Desdemona. Othello wishes to be left alone with his wife, he tells Emilia, ordering her to leave the room and guard the door. He then addresses Desdemona in a menacing tone, accusing her directly of disloyalty. Unable to contain his anguish, he eventually weeps tears of indignation.

Desdemona is perplexed. If the cause of his distress is the order to return to Venice, she says, he must not blame her; she will always take his side against her father.

Othello, lost in his own misery, takes no notice. He could cope if disease, poverty or captivity were inflicted on him, he claims: he can even tolerate the public mockery that will inevitably be his fate. But to lose his chance of love and his hopes for the future, and to discover that the object of that love is corrupt and hateful, is more than he can bear. Desdemona's beauty makes her wickedness all the more excruciating:

Othello: O thou weed
Who art so lovely fair and smell'st so sweet
That the sense aches at thee, would[1] thou hadst ne'er been born!
Desdemona: Alas, what ignorant sin have I committed?
Othello: Was this fair paper, this most goodly book
Made to write 'whore' upon? What committed!
Committed? O thou public commoner! [2]
... What committed!
Heaven stops the nose[3] at it ...

[1] *I wish*
[2] *prostitute*
[3] *holds its nose*

Furious that Desdemona will not admit her guilt, Othello storms out. As he passes Emilia, he warns her bluntly to keep quiet about anything she has witnessed.

> *Heaven stops the nose at it ...*
>
> Does Shakespeare's choice of words and images tell us anything about the personality, the likes and dislikes of the man himself? One twentieth-century scholar believed so:
>
> *"Shakespeare has clearly a very acute sense of smell, and is peculiarly sensitive to bad smells; the two he specially names and dislikes being the smell of unwashed humanity and of decaying corpses, both of them common enough in Elizabethan plague-stricken London ... it is above all in* Othello *that we are made conscious of the foul and horrible smell of evil ... the horror of the contrast between the fair looks of Desdemona and what he believes her deeds is made vivid by Othello entirely by means of smell."*
>
> Caroline Spurgeon, *Shakespeare's Imagery and What It Tells Us*, 1935

A cry for help

The shock of the encounter with Othello has left Desdemona exhausted. She asks Emilia to make her bed with the sheets from her wedding night, a reminder of the Othello who loved her. She also asks Emilia to bring Iago to her, hoping that he can shed some light on her husband's behaviour.

When Emilia returns with Iago, Desdemona cannot bring herself to repeat what Othello has said:

> *Iago:* What is the matter, lady?
> *Emilia:* Alas, Iago, my lord hath so bewhored her,[1]
> Thrown such despite and heavy terms[2] upon her
> That true hearts cannot bear it.
> *Desdemona:* Am I that name, Iago?
> *Iago:* What name, fair lady?

[1] *accused her of being a whore*
[2] *abuse and hurtful language*

Othello has called his wife a whore, repeats Emilia. At this, Desdemona starts weeping, and Iago comforts her.

Emilia is convinced that a malicious individual has persuaded the general of Desdemona's infidelity in order to gain some personal advantage.

The idea is ridiculous, says Iago dismissively. Emilia points out that he too was apparently taken in by a spiteful rumour about her own behaviour, and he becomes increasingly angry:

> *Emilia:* The Moor's abused by some most villainous knave,
> Some base notorious knave, some scurvy fellow.
> O heaven, that such companions thou'dst unfold[1]
> And put in every honest hand a whip …
> *Iago:* Speak within doors.[2]

Emilia: O fie upon them! Some such squire he was
That turned your wit the seamy side without [3]
And made you suspect me with the Moor.
Iago: You are a fool, go to.[4]

[1] *I wish you would reveal such fellows*
[2] *keep your voice down; keep your thoughts to yourself*
[3] *it was someone like that who turned your judgement inside out*
[4] *get out; shut up*

Desdemona implores Iago to talk to Othello and find out why he has become so hostile to her. She swears that she has never wronged him in any way, that she loves him and will never stop loving him. The very idea of being unfaithful to Othello horrifies her.

Iago reassures Desdemona that the general's ill temper is caused by affairs of state, but she is not convinced:

Desdemona: Unkindness may do much,
And his unkindness may defeat my life
But never taint my love. I cannot say whore:
It does abhor me now I speak the word;
To do the act that might the addition earn
Not the world's mass of vanity could make me.[1]
Iago: I pray you, be content, 'tis but his humour,[2]
The business of the state does him offence [3]
And he does chide with you.
Desdemona: If 'twere no other [4] –
Iago: 'Tis but so, I warrant.

[1] *all the world's riches would not persuade me to do the deed that would earn that title*
[2] *it's just the mood he's in*
[3] *distresses him*
[4] *if only that were all*

A trumpet sounds, summoning them to dinner: their guests from Venice are waiting. Iago hurries Desdemona away, reassuring her again that there is nothing to worry about.

Roderigo's last chance

Roderigo now comes to find Iago. He is by now at the end of his tether; he has no hope of winning Desdemona's love, he believes, and has wasted a great deal of time and money on his pointless quest. In particular, his precious gifts – given to Iago, and supposedly passed on to Desdemona – have had no effect:

Roderigo: … your words and performances are no kin together.[1]
Iago: You charge me most unjustly.
Roderigo: With nought but truth. I have wasted myself out of my means.[2] The jewels you have had from me to deliver to Desdemona would half have corrupted a votarist.[3] You have told me she hath received them, and returned me expectations and comforts of sudden respect and acquittance,[4] but I find none.

[1] *your deeds do not match your promises*
[2] *I have thrown away all my money*
[3] *nun*
[4] *you have come back with reassurances that I would soon be repaid with favourable attention from Desdemona*

Iago's attempts to calm Roderigo down only make him more impatient. Eventually Roderigo declares that he will abandon his pursuit of Desdemona: he will visit the lady himself, ask for his jewels to be returned, and apologise for his unwanted attentions.

Iago responds by congratulating Roderigo on standing up for himself. He has every right to be sceptical, concedes Iago, and this confrontational attitude shows his fighting spirit. Iago now promises, on pain of death, that Roderigo will be rewarded with Desdemona's love, and soon; but it will require all the courage and determination that Roderigo has just demonstrated.

Half a century after Shakespeare's death, tastes had changed. Although many of his plays were still popular, his work could seem unpolished and crude to contemporary audiences.

The most prominent female writer of the time complained that she was restricted by the more formal, refined conventions of her own age. In plays such as *Othello*, she argued, the strong language and violent passions were entirely justified:

"If I should repeat the Words exprest in these Scenes I mention, I might justly be charged with coarse ill Manners, and very little Modesty, and yet they so naturally fall into the places they are designed for, and so are proper for the Business, that there is not the least Fault to be found with them ..."

Aphra Behn, *The Luckey Chance*, 1687

Roderigo is uncertain, but asks to know more. Iago reveals that Othello is shortly to leave Cyprus for a far-off African country, and his place will be taken by Cassio. If Roderigo does not act quickly, Desdemona will slip out of his grasp for ever:

Iago: ... he goes into Mauretania and taketh away with him the fair Desdemona, unless his abode be lingered here [1] by some accident – wherein none can be so determinate [2] as the removing of Cassio.
Roderigo: How do you mean, removing of him?
Iago: Why, by making him uncapable of Othello's place: [3] knocking out his brains.
Roderigo: And that you would have me to do!
Iago: Ay, if you dare do yourself a profit and a right.

[1] *unless his stay here is prolonged*
[2] *no such accident would be more decisive*
[3] *unable to take Othello's place*

Cassio will be dining with his mistress this evening, and Iago intends to visit them. He will arrange for Cassio to leave at around midnight: Roderigo must be ready and waiting. Iago will be standing by to support him and ensure that Cassio is finished off.

Roderigo is not convinced, but Iago assures him that Cassio's death is essential. He promises to provide persuasive evidence:

Iago: … I will show you such a necessity in his death that you shall think yourself bound to put it on him. It is now high supper time, and the night grows to waste: about it.[1]

Roderigo: I will[2] hear further reason for this.

Iago: And you shall be satisfied.

[1] *it's getting late: get a move on*

[2] *I must, I demand to*

In 1964, Laurence Olivier famously played Othello with the newly-founded National Theatre company, in a production which formed the basis of a 1965 film. However, he had always regarded Iago as the more interesting role. Nearly thirty years earlier, he had taken an unorthodox approach to the part:

"I played Iago entirely for laughs. No menace, no danger at all. I thought, rather than play him like a sixteenth-century villainous character, it would be more interesting and acceptable to play him terribly sweet and as charming as could be. I felt that he would seem more dangerous and plausible this way …"

Laurence Olivier, *On Acting*, 1986

A sad song

IV, iii

The banquet held in honour of the visiting Venetians has just finished. Othello offers to walk home with Lodovico, one of the guests. Just before he leaves, he takes Desdemona aside, instructing her to go to bed immediately and to send her maidservant away.

Alone with Emilia, Desdemona mentions her husband's command. Not wishing to displease him, she intends to obey. As Emilia helps to prepare her mistress for bed, she makes no attempt to hide her unhappiness at what Othello has become. Desdemona's love, however, is undiminished:

Desdemona: … Give me my nightly wearing,[1] and adieu.
We must not now displease him.
Emilia: Ay. Would[2] you had never seen him!
Desdemona: So would not I: my love doth so approve him
That even his stubbornness, his checks,[3] his frowns
– Prithee unpin me[4] – have grace and favour.

[1] *nightclothes*
[2] *I wish*
[3] *rebukes*
[4] *unpin my hair*

Emilia says that, as requested, she has laid the sheets from Desdemona and Othello's wedding-night on their bed. Desdemona remarks that she would like to be wrapped in these sheets when she is buried, but Emilia dismisses the idea as idle chatter.

Still in a reflective mood, Desdemona mentions that an old song is going round her head, a song that her mother's maid used to sing. The maid had been deserted by the man she loved, and the song echoed her experience: in fact, she was singing it when she died.

Emilia, wanting to steer Desdemona's thoughts away from such gloomy subjects, mentions Lodovico, the visitor from Venice. He's an attractive man, she points out, hinting that he would have been a more suitable match for Desdemona:

Emilia: This Lodovico is a proper[1] man. A very handsome man.
Desdemona: He speaks well.
Emilia: I know a lady in Venice would have walked barefoot to Palestine[2] for a touch of his nether[3] lip.

[1] *admirable, courteous*
[2] *who would have gone on a long pilgrimage*
[3] *lower*

Desdemona, distracted by her thoughts, does not react. She starts singing the song of lost love that has been on her mind:

Desdemona: The poor soul sat sighing
by a sycamore tree,
Sing all a green willow:
Her hand on her bosom,
her head on her knee,
Sing willow, willow, willow.

At one point, she accidentally sings the wrong words, thinking of her own unwavering love for Othello. She corrects herself, remembering that the song is about blame and jealousy:

Desdemona: Let nobody blame him,
his scorn I approve[1] –
[*speaks*] Nay, that's not next …
I called my love false love;
but what said he then?
Sing willow, willow, willow:
If I court moe[2] women,
you'll couch[3] with moe men …

[1] *I don't mind his cruelty*
[2] *more*
[3] *go to bed*

> *"The scene is wonderfully effective and dramatically enriching in the contrasts it provides. In this masculine play, here is the talk of women ... In a play of noise, here is quietness; in among the violence, peace."*
>
> Levi Fox, *The Shakespeare Handbook*, 1987

Two views of morality

Desdemona now asks Emilia to leave her. However, the subject of sexual jealousy is playing on her mind, and she is keen to have Emilia's opinion before she leaves. In contrast to Desdemona's uncompromising attitude, her maid is more pragmatic and less serious:

Desdemona: O, these men, these men!
Dost thou in conscience think – tell me, Emilia –
That there be women do abuse their husbands
In such gross kind? [1]
Emilia: There be some such, no question.
Desdemona: Wouldst thou do such a deed for all the world?
Emilia: Why, would not you?
Desdemona: No, by this heavenly light!
Emilia: Nor I neither, by this heavenly light:
I might do't as well i'th' dark.
Desdemona: Wouldst thou do such a deed for all the world?
Emilia: The world's a huge thing: it is a great price
For a small vice.[2]

[1] *who deceive their husbands in such an appalling way*

[2] *a huge prize for a small sin*

Desdemona insists that Emilia, despite her flippant answers, would never be unfaithful to her husband in reality. In fact, she cannot imagine any woman behaving in such a way.

Emilia quickly becomes impatient with her mistress's unworldly attitude. Of course some women have affairs, she declares, pointing out that their husbands are often no better:

Emilia: But I do think it is their husbands' faults
If wives do fall. Say that they slack [1] their duties
And pour our treasures into foreign laps; [2]
Or else break out in peevish jealousies,
Throwing restraint upon us; [3] or say they strike us,
Or scant our former having in despite [4] …

[1] *neglect*
[2] *give their sexual favours to other women*
[3] *restricting our freedom*
[4] *reduce the amount of money they previously provided, out of spite*

Warming to her theme, Emilia asserts that husbands and wives should be held to the same standards. If men have appetites and weaknesses, the same is true for women. Husbands should not expect their wives to behave any more virtuously than they do themselves; if they are tempted to go astray, they should not be surprised if their wives do the same.

Emilia: Let husbands know
Their wives have sense like them: they see, and smell,
And have their palates both for sweet and sour
As husbands have.
… And have not we affections?
Desires for sport? And frailty, [1] as men have?
Then let them use [2] us well: else let them know,
The ills [3] we do, their ills instruct us so.

[1] *moral weakness, inability to resist temptation*
[2] *treat*
[3] *misdeeds, offences*

Desdemona disagrees. Rather than imitate other people's misconduct, she maintains, we should learn from it how to improve our own behaviour:

Desdemona: God me such usage send [1]
Not to pick bad from bad, but by bad mend! [2]

[1] *help me to make it my custom*
[2] *not to follow the example of evil behaviour, but to observe it and amend my own conduct*

Let husbands know
Their wives have sense like them ...

Emilia's heartfelt speech seems to have been added during revision of the play a few years after it was first created. This process was the result of pressure from an increasingly Puritanical government:

"In May 1606 an Act of Parliament to 'Restrain the Abuses of Players' became law. Designed to curb profanity in the theatre, it imposed a fine of £10 for every transgression ... soon after May 1606, Othello *and other plays were systematically trawled to remove oaths. The necessary rewrites involved changes of sense, metre, syntax and rhythm ... Shakespeare used the opportunity to tinker with* Othello, *making significant cuts and adding 150 lines, including a powerful new speech for Emilia at the end of Act IV which asserts the rights of women against the unkindness of men."*

Michael Wood, *In Search of Shakespeare*, 2005

A violent confrontation

It is late at night. In a street near Bianca's house, Iago is preparing Roderigo for the planned ambush. Cassio will be passing by very soon, and Roderigo must hold his nerve and strike without mercy:

Iago: … straight will he come.
Wear thy good rapier bare,[1] and put it home;[2]
Quick, quick, fear nothing, I'll be at thy elbow.
It makes or mars[3] us, think on that
And fix most firm thy resolution.

[1] *unsheathed, ready to use*
[2] *thrust it right in*
[3] *ruins*

Roderigo is uneasy, but Iago assures him he will be close at hand. Moving away, he remarks with satisfaction that he has successfully stirred up Roderigo's animosity towards Cassio. With luck, one or both of them will die in this encounter.

In any case, reflects Iago, they must both be killed soon. Roderigo has supplied him with lavish gifts of money and jewels, believing them to be for Desdemona; there is a danger he may demand them back, which must not be allowed to happen. As for Cassio:

Iago: If Cassio do remain
He hath a daily beauty[1] in his life
That makes me ugly; and besides, the Moor
May unfold me[2] to him – there stand I in much peril.
No, he must die.

[1] *ever-present courtesy and good looks*
[2] *disclose what I have said about Desdemona*

Cassio now approaches, and Roderigo lunges at him with his rapier. However, Cassio is wearing a thick, protective coat, and the blow is ineffective. He retaliates, wounding Roderigo severely. At the same time, Iago attacks Cassio from behind, stabbing him in the leg. He then runs off into the darkness, leaving both men injured and crying for help.

Othello now arrives on the scene. He recognises Cassio's voice calling desperately for help through the darkness. Believing that Cassio is dying, Othello assumes that Iago has carried out his promise to dispose of the lieutenant. He is all the more determined to follow Iago's example and punish Desdemona:

Othello: O brave Iago, honest and just,
That hast such noble sense of thy friend's wrong! [1]
Thou teachest me. Minion,[2] your dear [3] lies dead,
And your unblest fate hies [4] ...

[1] *sensitivity to the injustice done to me, your friend*
[2] *spoilt, pampered favourite; Desdemona*
[3] *Cassio*
[4] *your accursed destiny is approaching rapidly*

Lodovico and Gratiano, visitors from Venice, now come across the wounded men, both groaning in pain. In the darkness they cannot be sure how many men are present, and they suspect that they are being lured into a trap. While they are hesitating, Iago returns. He is dressed in his nightclothes, as if the disturbance had just woken him, and is carrying a lantern.

Cassio, hearing Iago's voice, cries out for help. He is unsure how many men attacked him, but he believes that at least one of them is nearby.

At this moment Roderigo calls out. Cassio identifies the voice as that of one of his assailants, and Iago immediately runs him through with his sword:

Roderigo: O, help me here!
Cassio: That's one of them.
Iago: O murderous slave! O villain!
[*stabs Roderigo*]
Roderigo: O damned Iago! O inhuman dog!

Iago now shouts out for assistance. He challenges the two bystanders, Lodovico and Gratiano: he then apologises, claiming not to have recognised them in the darkness and the confusion. He sets about dressing Cassio's wound.

Recriminations

Cassio's sweetheart Bianca now comes to find out what is causing all the commotion. She is devastated to discover that Cassio has been attacked.

As Bianca frantically tries to comfort Cassio, Iago publicly accuses her of involvement in the assault. He then feigns horror on finding Roderigo's corpse. The bystanders, also Venetians, are shocked:

Bianca: Alas, he faints! O Cassio, Cassio, Cassio!
Iago: Gentlemen all, I do suspect this trash [1]
To be a party [2] in this injury.
Patience awhile, good Cassio. Come, come,
Lend me a light. Know we this face, or no?
Alas, my friend and my dear countryman,
Roderigo? No – yes sure! – O heaven, Roderigo!
Gratiano: What, of Venice?
Iago: Even he, sir. Did you know him?
Gratiano: Know him? Ay.

[1] *worthless, disreputable woman*
[2] *participant, accomplice*

By now the uproar has roused the neighbourhood, and more people arrive on the scene. They prepare to carry Cassio away, urged on by Iago, who is determined to keep Bianca away from him and to cast suspicion on her. As Cassio leaves, Iago questions him about Roderigo:

Iago: [*to Bianca*] For you, mistress,
Save you your labour.[1] – He that lies slain here, Cassio,
Was my dear friend. [*to Cassio*] What malice was between you?[2]
Cassio: None in the world, nor do I know the man.
Iago: [*to Bianca*] What, look you pale?
… Behold her well, I pray you, look upon her:
Do you see, gentlemen? Nay, guiltiness will speak
Though tongues were out of use.[3]

[1] *don't waste your effort; leave Cassio alone*
[2] *between you and Roderigo*
[3] *guilt will always reveal itself in a person's expression, even if speech no longer existed*

Emilia is next to arrive. Iago orders Bianca to be arrested, and on hearing of the girl's possible involvement in the attack on Cassio, Emilia condemns her angrily:

Emilia: Alas, good gentleman! Alas, good Cassio!
Iago: This is the fruits of whoring.[1] Prithee, Emilia,
Go know of Cassio where he supped tonight.[2]
[*to Bianca*] What, do you shake at that?
Bianca: He supped at my house, but I therefore shake not.[3]
Iago: O, did he so? I charge you, go with me.
Emilia: O fie upon thee, strumpet![4]
Bianca: I am no strumpet
But of life as honest as you, that thus
Abuse me.

[1] *the consequence of spending time with prostitutes*
[2] *find out from Cassio where he had supper tonight*
[3] *I'm not shaking because of that*
[4] *slut, whore*

Iago warns Bianca that she will face further questioning. He then instructs Emilia to hurry away and tell Othello what has happened.

As the crowd disperses, Iago pauses for a final thought. The violent, chaotic events that have just happened, and those that are about to happen – the likely death of Cassio, and Othello's planned murder of Desdemona – may bring him success and security for life. On the other hand, they may lead to his ruin:

Iago: This is the night
That either makes me or fordoes me quite.[1]

[1] *makes my fortune or destroys me completely*

"Iago is the supreme test for those who will not see clearly ... He thinks more intensely than anyone else in the play. In fact, he has the mind of a playwright, manipulating people around his plots. When the plot gets out of hand, when the characters don't behave as expected, like a poor playwright he kills them off. Iago is the scourge of those whose thinking is muddled. He depends on their faulty vision to pervert reality."

Ben Okri, *A Way of Being Free*, 1997

Othello shows no mercy

V, ii

Othello is in his bedchamber, watching Desdemona as she sleeps, and preparing himself to take her life. It is justice that is driving him on, he tells himself, not his own desire for revenge. It is her adultery that has led to this:

Othello: It is the cause,[1] it is the cause, my soul!
Let me not name it to you, you chaste stars,
It is the cause. Yet I'll not shed her blood
Nor scar that whiter skin of hers than snow
And smooth as monumental alabaster:[2]
Yet she must die, else she'll betray more men.

1 *it is because of her crime*
2 *polished white stone used for funeral monuments*

All Othello needs to do, he reflects, is to blow out the candle and then extinguish Desdemona's life. However, her life, unlike a candle flame, cannot be restored:

Othello: But once put out thy light,
Thou cunning'st pattern of excelling nature,[1]
I know not where is that Promethean heat[2]
That can thy light relume[3] ...

1 *most intricate masterpiece of nature*
2 *divine fire, the property of the gods*
3 *reignite*

A rose, once plucked, cannot be given life again, he muses. With that thought he comes closer to Desdemona, inhaling her scent and kissing her sorrowfully.

But Othello remains resolute. Desdemona's death, while distressing, is necessary:

Othello: O balmy[1] breath, that dost almost persuade
Justice to break her sword! Once more, once more:
Be thus when thou art dead and I will kill thee
And love thee after. Once more, and that's the last.
[*kisses Desdemona*]
So sweet was ne'er so fatal. I must weep,
But they are cruel tears. This sorrow's heavenly,
It strikes where it doth love.[2]

[1] *fragrant*
[2] *it is like heaven's retribution, inflicted by God on those He loves*

Desdemona now awakes. Othello warns her that she must take this opportunity to pray for forgiveness of her sins. Confused and fearful, Desdemona vows that the only sin she has committed is her excessive love of Othello. Both his expression and his words are menacing:

Desdemona: And yet I fear you, for you're fatal[1] then
When your eyes roll so. Why I should fear I know not,
Since guiltiness I know not. But yet I feel I fear.
Othello: Think on thy sins.
Desdemona: They are loves I bear to you.[2]
Othello: Ay, and for that thou diest.
Desdemona: That death's unnatural that kills for loving.

[1] *threatening, intimidating*
[2] *my sins result from loving you too much*

Becoming more agitated, Othello raises the subject of the handkerchief that he gave to Desdemona as a love-token. He knows that she gave it to Cassio, he reveals. Desdemona fervently denies it, but Othello is unmoved. He cannot forget the scene, arranged by Iago, that he witnessed earlier: that of Cassio joking about Desdemona's devotion to him, followed by the arrival of Cassio's mistress, angrily flinging Desdemona's handkerchief back at him.

Desdemona's denial angers Othello; he has given her the chance to confess her sins, and she has failed to do so. He is determined that his action should be considered the just punishment of a sinner, not a vengeful act of violence. Cassio, he reveals, has been condemned by his own words:

Desdemona: I never did
Offend you in my life, never loved Cassio
But with such general warranty of heaven
As I might love:[1] I never gave him token.
Othello: By heaven, I saw my handkerchief in's hand!
O perjured[2] woman, thou dost stone my heart[3]
And makest me call what I intend to do
A murder, which I thought a sacrifice!
I saw the handkerchief.
Desdemona: He found it then,
I never gave it to him. Send for him hither,
Let him confess the truth.
Othello: He hath confessed.

[1] *with the love that heaven encourages us to feel*
[2] *dishonest, caught in the act of lying*
[3] *turn my heart to stone, make me merciless*

Desdemona is horrified to hear that Othello has ordered Iago to kill Cassio. Her tears enrage Othello even further and, unmoved by her pleas, he forces her down onto the bed and suffocates her:

Othello: Out, strumpet, weep'st thou for him to my face?
Desdemona: O, banish me, my lord, but kill me not!
Othello: Down, strumpet!
Desdemona: Kill me tomorrow, let me live tonight!
Othello: Nay, if you strive[1] –
Desdemona: But half an hour!
Othello: Being done,[2] there is no pause –
Desdemona: But while I say one prayer!
Othello: It is too late.

[1] *struggle*
[2] *now that the decision has been made*

The truth is revealed

Suddenly, shouting is heard at the door. Emilia has come with urgent news. Othello hesitates; he wants to be certain that Desdemona is dead before letting her maidservant in. Becoming aware of the enormity of Desdemona's death, he struggles to control his emotions:

Othello: Ha, no more moving?
Still as the grave. Shall she come in? Were't good?
I think she stirs again. No – what's best to do?
If she come in, she'll sure speak to my wife.
My wife, my wife! What wife? I have no wife.
O insupportable, O heavy hour!
Methinks it should be now a huge eclipse
Of sun and moon, and that th'affrighted globe
Should yawn at alteration.[1]

[1] *this sudden change should cause earthquakes to split open the surface of the terrified Earth*

Drawing the curtains across the bed to hide Desdemona's body, Othello unlocks the door. Emilia immediately tells him the dreadful news: there has been a murder in the streets.

Othello feigns surprise, suggesting that recent irregularities in the course of the moon may have caused an outbreak of madness. In reality, he is confident that she means the killing of Cassio, carried out by Iago, which he believed he witnessed earlier. He is taken aback to hear that Cassio is still alive:

Emilia: Cassio, my lord, hath killed
A young Venetian, called Roderigo.
Othello: Roderigo killed? And Cassio killed?
Emilia: No, Cassio is not killed.
Othello: Not Cassio killed?
Then murder's out of tune,[1] and sweet revenge
Grows harsh.

[1] *inharmonious, discordant*

At this moment a voice is heard, claiming that Cassio has done nothing wrong. It is Desdemona: on the verge of death, she is able to utter a few words, and her mistress immediately recognises her voice.

Emilia rushes over to the bed and pulls back the curtain. With her last words, Desdemona declares her innocence, and refuses to blame anyone for her death:

Emilia: Help, help, ho, help! O lady, speak again,
Sweet Desdemona, O sweet mistress, speak!
Desdemona: A guiltless death I die.
Emilia: O, who hath done
This deed?
Desdemona: Nobody. I myself. Farewell.
Commend me to my kind lord – O farewell!

The diarist Samuel Pepys recorded that, during a performance of *Othello* in 1660, *"a very pretty lady that sat by me, called out, to see Desdemona smothered."* The suffocation of Desdemona can be a powerful, distressing scene, and there are numerous accounts of audience members fainting, crying out, and even interrupting the action:

"These anecdotes may not all be true, but they reveal a desire for agency on the audience's part: a desire to protect Desdemona from an unjust death ... the audience knows much more than Othello and is therefore placed in the position of either being complicit with the tragic action (i.e., by watching silently and doing nothing) or attempting to thwart that tragedy ..."

Ayanna Thompson, Introduction to the Arden edition of *Othello*, 2016

At first, Othello denies involvement in Desdemona's death, claiming that her words prove him to be innocent. However, unable to contain his feelings, he then goes on to denounce her angrily. Emilia is outraged:

Othello: She's like a liar gone to burning hell:
'Twas I that killed her.
Emilia: O, the more angel she,
And you the blacker devil!
Othello: She turned to folly, and she was a whore.
Emilia: Thou dost belie[1] her, and thou art a devil.
Othello: She was false[2] as water.
Emilia: Thou art rash as fire to say
That she was false. O, she was heavenly true!

[1] *slander*
[2] *changeable, deceitful*

Othello insists that the killing was justifiable; if not, it would have been a terrible crime. When he mentions that Iago was involved in proving that Cassio and Desdemona were having an illicit affair, Emilia's suspicions are immediately aroused:

Othello: Cassio did top[1] her: ask thy husband else.[2]
O, I were damned beneath all depth in hell
But that I did proceed upon just grounds[3]
To this extremity. Thy husband knew it all.
Emilia: My husband?

[1] *copulate with*
[2] *if you don't believe me*
[3] *if I didn't have a valid cause for such drastic action*

Emilia is appalled both by Othello's violent act and by the dreadful possibility that her husband may have planted a false story in the general's mind. Othello insists that Iago is utterly trustworthy:

Othello: … 'twas he that told me on her first;[1]
An honest man he is, and hates the slime
That sticks on filthy deeds.
Emilia: My husband!

[1] *who first informed me about her*

Convinced of Desdemona's innocence, Emilia angrily alleges that her only fault was to fall in love with such an evil, unworthy character. Othello in turn becomes angry, and tries to silence her. Undeterred, she calls out for help:

Othello: Peace, you were best![1]
Emilia: Thou hast not half that power to do me harm
As I have to be hurt.[2] O gull,[3] O dolt,
As ignorant as dirt! Thou hast done a deed
[*Othello threatens her with his sword*]
– I care not for thy sword, I'll make thee known
Though[4] I lost twenty lives. Help, help, ho, help!
The Moor hath killed my mistress! Murder, murder!

1 *it would be best for you if you kept quiet*
2 *to endure pain*
3 *fool, dupe*
4 *even if*

Emilia speaks out

Hearing Emilia's cries, Montano, Gratiano and Iago rush in. Emilia immediately confronts her husband: she must know the truth, even though she dreads what she might hear. Iago's reply is evasive:

Emilia: Disprove this villain,[1] if thou be'st a man;
He says thou told'st him that his wife was false,
I know thou didst not, thou'rt not such a villain.
Speak, for my heart is full.
Iago: I told him what I thought, and told no more
Than what he found himself was apt[2] and true.

1 *contradict what Othello has said*
2 *credible, likely*

Eventually Iago admits that he told Othello of Desdemona's infidelity with Cassio. He orders Emilia to keep quiet, but she responds furiously, revealing to the shocked onlookers that this falsehood has led to Desdemona's death:

Emilia: You told a lie, an odious, damned lie!
Upon my soul, a lie, a wicked lie!
She false with Cassio? Did you say with Cassio?
Iago: With Cassio, mistress. Go to, charm[1] your tongue.
Emilia: I will not charm my tongue, I am bound to speak:
My mistress here lies murdered in her bed.

[1] *control*

Othello confesses that he has killed Desdemona with his own hands, and he throws himself on the bed in anguish. He remains adamant, however, that he was motivated by her adultery.

Gratiano now breaks the news that Desdemona's father Brabantio has died. Perhaps it is for the best, says Gratiano: her father was already unhappy at her marriage, and hearing that his daughter had died would have driven him to commit a mortal sin.

Othello continues with his attempt to justify himself. The situation is tragic, he admits, but he has seen irrefutable proof of Desdemona's wrongdoing:

Othello: 'Tis pitiful; but yet Iago knows
That she with Cassio hath the act of shame
A thousand times committed. Cassio confessed it,
And she did gratify[1] his amorous works
With that recognizance[2] and pledge of love
Which I first gave her: I saw it in his hand,
It was a handkerchief …

[1] *reward*
[2] *token, reminder*

... she with Cassio hath the act of shame
A thousand times committed.

One unsettling aspect of *Othello* is the changeable, elusive nature of time in the play. On the one hand, events move with unnerving speed; the action of the play covers two or three days at the most. On the other hand, there are frequent suggestions of a longer, more detailed backdrop to events.

Many scholars have pondered this issue of 'double time': was it a deliberate decision on Shakespeare's part, or an unconscious choice? Or even a simple error? Has the original play been cut or amended in some way? In the theatre, however, the pace and tension of the drama are so compelling that we are unlikely to be troubled by such questions.

Emilia immediately realises what has happened: this is the handkerchief that she found on the floor, and which her husband had snatched from her hand. He must somehow have arranged for it to be in Cassio's possession.

Iago tries desperately to silence his wife: if the truth emerges, his plans will have come to nothing, and his life will be utterly destroyed. Emilia demands to be heard:

Emilia: O God, O heavenly God!
Iago: Zounds, hold your peace!
Emilia: 'Twill out,[1] 'twill out! I peace?
No, I will speak as liberal as the north.[2]
Let heaven and men and devils, let them all,
All, all cry shame against me, yet[3] I'll speak.
Iago: Be wise, and get you home.

[1] *the truth will become known*
[2] *as freely as the wind*
[3] *still*

Finally Iago draws out his sword and lunges at Emilia. Gratiano restrains him, and he hurls insults at her as she proclaims the truth:

Emilia: O thou dull[1] Moor, that handkerchief thou speak'st of
I found by fortune[2] and did give my husband,
For often, with a solemn earnestness
– More than indeed belonged to such a trifle –
He begged of me to steal't.
Iago: Villainous whore!
Emilia: She give it Cassio? No, alas, I found it
And I did give't my husband.
Iago: Filth, thou liest!
Emilia: By heaven I do not, I do not, gentlemen!

[1] *ignorant*
[2] *chance*

In an instant, everything becomes clear to Othello. He rushes violently at Iago, determined to kill him. In the ensuing struggle, Iago breaks free from his captors, stabs Emilia and runs out of the room.

Iago survives

Emilia, fatally wounded, asks to be laid by Desdemona's side. Meanwhile, Montano grabs Othello's sword. Giving it to Gratiano, he orders him to stand outside and guard the door: Othello must be killed rather than allowed to escape. Montano himself sets off to find Iago.

The loss of his sword is fitting, reflects Othello, broken by the knowledge that he has lost everything: his love, his integrity, his reputation.

Emilia, lying next to her mistress's body, remembers the song that was on Desdemona's mind before she died. She sings a fragment of it, and as she dies she reproaches Othello once again for mistrusting his wife:

Emilia: What did thy song bode,[1] lady?
Hark, canst thou hear me? I will play the swan
And die in music.[2] [*sings*] Willow, willow, willow.

– Moor, she was chaste, she loved thee, cruel Moor,
So come my soul to bliss [3] as I speak true!
So speaking as I think, alas, I die.

[1] *mean, foretell*
[2] *like the swan, I will sing just before I die*
[3] *may my soul go to heaven*

Othello, deep in his own thoughts, suddenly remembers that he keeps a sword in the bedchamber. He finds it, and calls Gratiano back into the room.

Believing him to be unarmed, Gratiano comes in. He is startled to see that the general has a weapon, but Othello assures him that he is in no danger. His life as a warrior has come to an end:

Othello: I have seen the day
That with this little arm and this good sword
I have made my way through more impediments
Than twenty times your stop [1] …
… 'Tis not so now.
Be not afraid, though you do see me weaponed: [2]
Here is my journey's end, here is my butt [3]
And very sea-mark of my utmost sail.[4]

[1] *your power to stop me*
[2] *armed*
[3] *goal, end; in archery, a target*
[4] *the beacon marking the entrance to my final harbour*

Approaching Desdemona's lifeless body, Othello is overcome with grief and self-loathing:

Othello: O cursed, cursed slave!
Whip me, ye devils,
From the possession of this heavenly sight!
Blow me about in winds, roast me in sulphur,
Wash me in steep-down [1] gulfs of liquid fire!
O Desdemon! Dead, Desdemon. Dead! O, O!

[1] *sheer, precipitous*

At this point Montano and his officers return, bringing Iago, now their prisoner. With them is the nobleman Lodovico: and Cassio, still unable to walk after his injury, is carried into the room.

Lodovico calls for Othello and Iago to come forward. Before the others have time to disarm him, Othello stabs Iago, condemning him as a devil. Iago replies, tauntingly, that he may be right:

Othello: I look down towards his feet, but that's a fable.[1]
If that thou be'st a devil, I cannot kill thee.[2]
[*stabs Iago*]

Lodovico: Wrench his sword from him.
Iago: I bleed, sir, but not killed.

[1] *he does not have cloven hooves, but that is just a myth; he may still be a devil*
[2] *it was supposedly impossible to kill a devil*

Lodovico asks Othello about the plan to kill Cassio, and he admits his guilt. Iago, however, flatly refuses to co-operate any further. His motives will remain forever unknown:

Lodovico: This wretch hath part confessed his villainy.
Did you and he consent in Cassio's death?
Othello: Ay.
Cassio: Dear general, I never gave you cause.
Othello: I do believe it, and I ask your pardon.
Will you, I pray, demand that demi-devil
Why he hath thus ensnared my soul and body?
Iago: Demand me nothing. What you know, you know.
From this time forth I never will speak word.

Demand me nothing. What you know, you know.

"Shakespeare has no intention of letting the audience off the hook ... Iago talks directly to us throughout the play and takes us into his confidence, assuming that we share his views, understand his reasoning and admire his ingenuity ... we can be sure every word of that barbed line is addressed, disconcertingly, to us too."

Kiernan Ryan, *Racism, misogyny and 'motiveless malignity' in* Othello, 2016

A last kiss

Lodovico announces that two letters have been discovered in Roderigo's pockets. One is from Iago, urging him to kill Cassio. The other, written by Roderigo himself and never sent, complains of his mistreatment by Iago, and mentions the fact that Iago had instructed him to start the brawl which resulted in Cassio's dismissal.

It has also come to light that the handkerchief that inflamed Othello's jealousy so powerfully was left in Cassio's lodgings by Iago: in fact, Iago has been behind all the events that have led to the present catastrophe.

Othello is now formally removed as governor of Cyprus, to be replaced by Cassio. He is to be held in prison, Lodovico tells him, until the Venetian state makes a decision about his future. As for Iago, the most severe punishment possible must be meted out:

Lodovico: You must forsake this room and go with us.
Your power and your command is taken off
And Cassio rules in Cyprus. For this slave,
If there be any cunning cruelty
That can torment him much and hold him long,[1]
It shall be his.

[1] *keep him alive for as long as possible while he suffers*

Before he is taken away, Othello makes a request to his captors. He asks that, in their reports to the authorities in Venice, they describe him and his actions impartially. He realises that his military prowess no longer counts for anything, but he wants the world to know that he was driven to his terrible crime by extremes of passion:

Othello: Soft you,[1] a word or two before you go.
I have done the state some service, and they know't:
No more of that. I pray you, in your letters,
When you shall these unlucky[2] deeds relate,
Speak of me as I am. Nothing extenuate,
Nor set down aught in malice.[3] Then must you speak
Of one that loved not wisely, but too well;
Of one not easily jealous, but, being wrought,[4]
Perplexed in the extreme …

1 *wait a moment*
2 *unfortunate, fateful*
3 *do not tone down the gravity of my offence, but do not write anything deliberately malicious*
4 *worked on, manipulated*

Othello now recalls an episode in which he defended the honour of Christian Venice against an adversary:

Othello: … in Aleppo once,
Where a malignant and a turbanned Turk
Beat a Venetian and traduced[1] the state,
I took by th' throat the circumcised dog
And smote him – thus!

1 *insulted, slandered*

Soft you, a word or two before you go.

"Othello's speech … shows that the Ancient has not, after all, ensnared the hero's soul. Enough of the servant of the Venetian republic survives to enable Othello to reaffirm the values by which he once lived and to execute justice on himself."

G. R. Hibbard, Othello *and the Pattern of Shakespearean Tragedy*, 1968

At this moment, to the horror of his onlookers, Othello pulls out a dagger and stabs himself. He then staggers to the bed on which Desdemona's body lies, and kisses her as he too dies.

Cassio had feared that the general might try to take his own life rather than live with the knowledge of what he has done:

Othello: I kissed thee ere[1] I killed thee: no way but this,[2]
Killing myself, to die upon a kiss.
Cassio: This did I fear, but thought he had no weapon,
For he was great of heart.

[1] *before*
[2] *this is the only way left to me*

Lodovico turns to Iago accusingly: this death too is his work. He orders the curtains to be drawn, to hide the dreadful sight of the bodies of Desdemona, Emilia and Othello. Cassio, as the new governor of Cyprus, will be responsible for Iago's punishment:

Lodovico: To you, lord governor,
Remains the censure[1] of this hellish villain,
The time, the place, the torture: O, enforce it!
Myself will straight aboard,[2] and to the state
This heavy act with heavy heart relate.

[1] *judgement, sentencing*
[2] *I will board a ship immediately*

Lodovico will return to Venice: the senate must be informed of the tragic events, set in motion by Iago, that have unfolded, so swiftly and so inexorably, on the island of Cyprus.

Acknowledgements

The following publications have proved invaluable as sources of factual information and critical insight:

- John F. Andrews, *Perspectives on* Othello, Everyman, 1995
- W. H. Auden, *The Dyer's Hand*, Faber & Faber, 1963
- Anne Barton, *Hell and Night*, Herald Press, 1979
- Jonathan Bate, *Soul of the Age*, Penguin, 2009
- Charles Boyce, *Shakespeare A to Z*, Roundtable Press, 1990
- A. C. Bradley, *Shakespearean Tragedy*, Macmillan, 1904
- Richard Dutton, *William Shakespeare: A Literary Life*, Macmillan, 1989
- Alison Findlay, *Women in Shakespeare*, Bloomsbury Arden Shakespeare, 2014
- Nicholas Fogg, *Hidden Shakespeare*, Amberley Publishing, 2013
- Levi Fox, *The Shakespeare Handbook*, Bodley Head, 1987
- Germaine Greer, *Shakespeare*, Oxford University Press, 1986
- John Gross, *After Shakespeare*, Oxford University Press, 2002
- G. R. Hibbard, Othello *and the Pattern of Shakespearean Tragedy*, Cambridge University Press, 1968
- E. A. J. Honigmann, Introduction to *Othello* in the Arden Shakespeare Third Series, 1999
- Jan Kott, *Shakespeare Our Contemporary*, Doubleday, 1965
- F. R. Leavis, *Diabolic Intellect and the Noble Hero*, Cambridge University Press, 1937
- Maynard Mack, *Everybody's Shakespeare*, Bison Books, 1993

- Ben Okri, *A Way of Being Free*, Phoenix House, 1997
- Laurence Olivier, *On Acting*, Weidenfeld & Nicolson, 1986
- Kiernan Ryan, *Racism, misogyny and 'motiveless malignity' in* Othello, Bloomsbury, 2016
- Jessica Slights, Introduction to *Othello*, Internet Shakespeare Editions, University of Victoria, 2018
- Susan Snyder, Othello *and the Conventions of Romantic Comedy*, Princeton University Press, 1972
- Caroline Spurgeon, *Shakespeare's Imagery and What It Tells Us*, Cambridge University Press, 1935
- Gary Taylor, *Reinventing Shakespeare*, Hogarth Press, 1990
- Ayanna Thompson, Introduction to *Othello* in the Arden Shakespeare Third Series (revised edition), 2016
- John Wain, *The Living World of Shakespeare*, Macmillan, 1964
- Michael Wood, *In Search of Shakespeare*, BBC Books, 2005

Guides currently available in the *Shakespeare Handbooks* series are:

- **Antony & Cleopatra** (ISBN 978 1 899747 02 3)
- **As You Like It** (ISBN 978 1 899747 00 9)
- **The Comedy of Errors** (ISBN 978 1 899747 16 0)
- **Coriolanus** (ISBN 978 1 899747 21 4)
- **Cymbeline** (ISBN 978 1 899747 20 7)
- **Hamlet** (ISBN 978 1 899747 07 8)
- **Henry IV, Part 1** (ISBN 978 1 899747 05 4)
- **Henry IV, Part 2** (ISBN 978 1 899747 25 2)
- **Julius Caesar** (ISBN 978 1 899747 11 5)
- **King Lear** (ISBN 978 1 899747 03 0)
- **Love's Labour's Lost** (ISBN 978 1 899747 23 8)
- **Macbeth** (ISBN 978 1 899747 04 7)
- **Measure for Measure** (ISBN 978 1 899747 14 6)
- **The Merchant of Venice** (ISBN 978 1 899747 13 9)
- **The Merry Wives of Windsor** (ISBN 978 1 899747 18 4)
- **A Midsummer Night's Dream** (ISBN 978 1 899747 09 2)
- **Much Ado About Nothing** (ISBN 978 1 899747 17 7)
- **Othello** (ISBN 978 1 899747 12 2)
- **Pericles** (ISBN 978 1 899747 24 5)
- **Richard II** (ISBN 978 1 899747 19 1)
- **Richard III** (ISBN 978 1 899747 22 1)
- **Romeo & Juliet** (ISBN 978 1 899747 10 8)
- **The Tempest** (ISBN 978 1 899747 08 5)
- **Twelfth Night** (ISBN 978 1 899747 01 6)
- **The Winter's Tale** (ISBN 978 1 899747 15 3)

www.shakespeare-handbooks.com

www.ingramcontent.com/pod-product-compliance
Lightning Source LLC
Chambersburg PA
CBHW061753020426
42331CB00006B/1469

* 9 7 8 1 8 9 9 7 4 7 1 2 2 *